To Sam

December 1987 —

One of these days you may
be at the stick — well maybe
you'll fly a great model (after
you build it)

Love,
Aunt Sue & Uncle Charles

MODERN JET AIRCRAFT

MODERN JET AIRCRAFT

MICHAEL J H TAYLOR

PARK SOUTH BOOKS

A Bison Book

Published by Park South Books
An imprint of Publishers Marketing Enterprises Inc.
386 Park Avenue South
New York, New York 10016

Produced by Bison Books Corp.
17 Sherwood Place
Greenwich, CT 06830
USA

ISBN 0 86124 170 3

Printed in Hong Kong

Reprinted 1986

CONTENTS

Although this book is based upon *Modern Jet Aircraft*, to appreciate fully the advancement of today's jets it is useful, perhaps, to have some understanding of their ancestors that appeared in the skies of the 1940s and 50s.

Power Jets Ltd, the first company in the world to run a turbojet engine designed for aircraft propulsion, had originally intended to apply its engine to a futuristic stratospheric mailplane. In the event the first flyable Power Jets engine was installed in the military-designated Gloster E.28/39 experimental aircraft and subsequent production engines from Rolls-Royce were used to power Britain's first operational jet fighters, Gloster Meteor F.Mk 1s. It is reasonable, therefore, that the first section of this chapter be devoted to early jet fighters.

Britain's Meteor was, in many respects, conventional. It had an oval-section, all-metal stressed-skin fuselage constructed with an integral wing center section. The two Rolls-Royce Welland I turbojets, each rated at 771kg (1700lb) static thrust, were mounted near the extremities of the wing center section and so were within the complete tapering wings. Armament comprised four 20mm British Hispano

Nearly one-third of all Gloster Meteor jet fighters produced were of the F.Mk 8 version, which featured an ejection seat for the pilot.

cannon and a camera gun was carried in the nose. The first Meteors went to No 616 Squadron, RAF, which became operational on 27 July 1944. That first day No 616 began operations against V-1 flying-bombs launched at Britain, the first two being destroyed on 4 August when one was tipped over by the wing of a Meteor which flew alongside and the second by cannon fire. The maximum speed of this first Allied jet was 676km/h (420mph).

The wartime Meteor F.Mk 2 prototype and F.Mk 3 operational aircraft were powered by Goblin and Derwent I (all but 15 of 280 built) engines respectively, the latter attaining a speed of 793km/h (493mph). The Meteor F.Mk 4 with Derwent 5 engines, reduced wing span, and other refinements which included a pressurized cockpit, became the first postwar version. On 7 November 1945 one F.Mk 4 established the first official world speed record for aircraft since 1939, achieving 975.67km/h (606.25mph). Subsequent versions of the Meteor included variants for the roles of fighter-reconnaissance, two-seat training, two-seat night fighting and unarmed high-altitude reconnaissance. The NF.Mk 11 was the first jet night fighter to enter

RAF service, in 1951, but the major production version of the Meteor was the F.Mk 8, which made up nearly one-third of the total of about 3550 Meteors built. Meteors were also flown by the air forces of 11 other countries.

The German rival to the Meteor was the Messerschmitt Me 262, although it is believed that no Meteor and Me 262 ever met in the skies above Europe. This twin-jet fighter, which secured orders to equip the Luftwaffe, was chosen for production in preference to the rival Heinkel He 280 and went on to prove an excellent aircraft. Interestingly, it was upon the Me 262 that Czechoslovakia based its postwar S-92 fighter and CS-92 fighter-bomber. The first Me 262 to fly on turbojet power alone was Me 262V3. This made its first flight on 18 July 1942, on the power of two 840kg (1852lb) st Junkers Jumo 109-004A turbojet engines. But, by then more than a year had passed since the first flight had taken place of the turbojet-powered He 280.

Of the 30 preproduction Me 262s ordered, the first dozen were used in various tests. The remainder, however, became true Me 262A-0s and many were delivered to the specially formed evaluation unit Erprobungskommando 262 from April 1944, which subsequently also received the first full-production Me 262A-1a Schwalbe (Swallow) fighters. This unit 'downed' the first Allied aircraft destroyed by jets, during a

series of experimental interceptions, but on 25 July an Me 262 was lost in an attack on an RAF Mosquito. On 28 August, American Republic P-47 Thunderbolt fighters of the 78th Fighter Group shot down an Me 262A-2a Sturmvogel (Stormbird), the first jet to be destroyed in air combat. This jet had been one of the few aircraft attached to KG 51 Kommando Schenck, which had moved to Juvincourt on 10 July to begin operations over France. The Me 262A-2a itself was the fighter-bomber variant of the Me 262, produced at Hitler's insistence with provision for two 250kg or one 500kg bomb. It was not until November of 1944 that Hitler took notice of his advisors and restored the fighter variant as the main production version. By the end of the war only about 200 of the 1433 Me 262s built had become operational, although Germany boasted more than ten 'jet aces'. Indeed Oberstleutnant Heinz Bar of JV 44 destroyed 16 Allied aircraft while piloting the Me 262.

Like the Meteor, the Me 262 used two turbojet engines, in the form of 900kg (1984lb) st Junkers Jumo 004Bs installed in nacelles below the marginally swept wings. Armament was four 30mm MK 108 cannon and the maximum speed was an impressive 868km/h (539mph).

A second, simpler German jet fighter became operational as the war in Europe was coming to a close, but one

which had only minor impact. By September 1944 Germany's plight was getting daily more desperate, its ground forces on the retreat and its manufacturing plant, communications and cities under 24 hour attack from American and British bombers. At the beginning of September it was decided in Germany that a new jet fighter was required that could be produced in vast quantities quickly by semi-skilled workers overseeing forced and voluntary unskilled labor, one which could be constructed from available materials and needed only a single engine, but was nevertheless capable of a speed of at least 750km/h (466mph). Only a few days was allowed for initial proposals. Having been banned from further work on jet aircraft after its He 280, Heinkel was anxious to be awarded the contract and, indeed, was in a strong position: the company had already worked on the idea of a lightweight fighter under the name Spatz (Sparrow). The Spatz formed the basis of the Project 1073 which, on 23 September, was selected for production by the RLM under its Volksjäger (People's Fighter) program.

Had the Volksjäger project met its original aims, it would have been one of the major German achievements of the war. Goering envisioned thousands of members of the Hitler Youth becoming Germany's new fighter pilots, progressing from initial flight training on gliders to the Volksjäger with little or

no intermediate powered flight training. The fighter itself was to be produced in conventional factories and in underground works inside salt and potassium mines.

Heinkel's Volksjäger was known as the He 162 Salamander, the prototype of which flew for the first time at Vienna-Schwechat on 6 December 1944. The second flight ended in tragedy, when the prototype lost the leading-edge and tip of one wing and an aileron. The pilot was killed. Examination showed that the aircraft's wooden wings with metal tips were not at fault but that the bonding used had deteriorated the wood. This was an easy fault to rectify.

The He 162 proved a difficult fighter to fly and would have been a totally unsuitable mount for Goering's young pilots. To keep the structure simple and light, the BMW 003E turbojet engine was mounted on the top of the fuselage, exhausting forward of and between a twin tail unit. However, it easily met the RLM's speed requirement, reaching 840km/h (522mph). It could climb to 6000m (19,685ft) in just over 6.5 minutes and carried a reasonable 'punch', with two 20mm MG 151 cannon.

Although the plan had been to produce 50 He 162s in January 1945, double that number in February and thereafter building up to 1000 per month, production fell dramatically

Above: An abandoned Messerschmitt Me 262. Produced in both fighter and fighter-bomber variants, the Me 262 demonstrated higher performance than Britain's Meteor.

short of these targets. Indeed, only a handful of aircraft were ready for delivery by the end of January. On 3 May Salamanders were among the aircraft abandoned by the retreating Germans at Salzburg and by the end of the war only Einsatz-Gruppe JG 1 was so equipped, having managed little flying with the 50 aircraft in its possession since 4 May. Perhaps 116 of the 250 to 300 Salamanders completed had been received by the Luftwaffe by the time of Germany's capitulation, and then flown only by experienced Luftwaffe pilots.

The Bell XP-59A Airacomet, the first American turbojet-powered airplane to fly, on 1 October 1942, was the subject of limited production orders. Thirteen service evaluation YP-59As were delivered in 1943, followed by twenty P-59As with General Electric I-16 or J31-GE-3 engines and thirty P-59Bs. The latter were the most powerful, each using two 907kg (2000lb)st J31-GE-5 engines to achieve 665km/h (413mph). Entering USAAF service from August 1944, they were America's first operational jet aircraft.

The honor of being the first American jet in service as a fighter did not go to the Airacomet, however, as it was used

Below: Germany's People's Fighter, the Heinkel He 162A-2 Volksjäger, intended to be mass produced in conventional factories and in underground works inside salt and potassium mines and perhaps piloted by little-trained members of the Hitler Youth.

Left: Flying in echelon formation are two of the thirteen Bell YP-59A Airacomet jet fighters ordered for the USAF.

mainly as jet fighter trainer. This accolade went to the Lockheed P-80 Shooting Star, which was also America's first single-engined jet fighter. The Shooting Star was the result of a request made in mid-1943 to the Lockheed Aircraft Corporation for a new single-seat fighter based around the British de Havilland H-1 turbojet engine. In fact an H-1 engine had arrived in America from Britain in July. Only 180 days were allowed for completion of the prototype Shooting Star, but Lockheed pulled out all the stops to get the XP-80 prototype in the air in 143 days, on 8 January 1944.

In many respects the XP-80 was the first of the modern jet fighters, lacking swept wings and other sophistications of later fighters but with its engine installed within the fuselage center-section, fed with air via fuselage intakes forward of the wing roots.

It had been intended that the Allis-Chalmers Company would put the H-1 into mass production in America. When this proved impossible a change of plans had to be made for the two XP-80A prototypes and thirteen YP-80A service evaluation aircraft already under contract. The delays this caused meant that the first XP-80A did not fly until mid-1944, using the 1700kg (3750lb) static thrust of a General Electric I-40. The I-40 installed was, in fact, only the fourth development example of this engine and the first to become airborne. Evolved from the I-16, the I-40 had only been completed in prototype form in January of that year.

The YP-80As were fitted with General Electric J33-GE-9 or -11 engines and carried six 0.50in machine-guns each. These fighters found their way into USAAF service from October 1944 and two were sent to Europe. The first full production version was the P-80A, each installed with an Allison J33 turbojet. Too late for war service, they began equipping the USAAF from December 1945. Other versions followed, including the famous T-33 two-

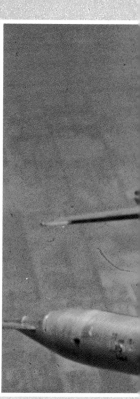

Below: The second of two Lockheed XP-80A Shooting Star jet fighter prototypes, fitted with a General Electric I-40 turbojet engine.

Right: The final production version of the Lockheed Starfire was the F-94C, armed with 24 Mighty Mouse air-to-air rockets in the nose (carried around the radome) and a similar number of rockets in two wing-mounted pods.

seat trainer derivative plus naval trainer versions. Related to the tandem two-seat T-33A was Lockheed's later F-94 Starfire, which entered USAF service from mid-1950 as its first all-weather jet fighter. Meanwhile it was to a USAF 'C' series Shooting Star that went the historical record of the first destruction of a jet fighter by another jet in combat, achieved on 8 November 1950 during the Korean War. The aircraft shot down was a Chinese-flown Mikoyan-Gurevich MiG-15, a highly successful swept-wing Soviet fighter that had its US equivalent in the North American F-86 Sabre. The first production F-86A Sabres went to the 1st Fighter Group, USAF, from February 1949 as that service's first swept-wing jet.

Returning briefly to the Second World War, the prototype of Britain's second jet fighter, and the RAF's first with a single turbojet engine, flew for the first time on 20 September 1943 as the de Havilland DH.100 Vampire. Power was provided by an early form of Goblin turbojet, installed in the rear of the aircraft's short fuselage nacelle to exhaust between and under a twin-boom tail unit. Production examples of this single-seater did not enter RAF service until 1946. Subsequent versions of the Vampire included the NF.Mk 10 two-seat night fighter and Sea Vampire, the latter becoming the Fleet Air Arm's

first jet fighter. Interestingly, a Vampire was the first pure jet to land and take-off from an aircraft carrier (HMS *Ocean* on 3 December 1945). The Vampire was also exported and built under license abroad; French-built FB.Mk 5s and the similar SNCASE Mistral (constructed from locally produced materials) were the first operational jets in France.

The aircraft detailed to this point were the most important early jet fighters, all subsonic and the ancestors of later supersonic types. There were, as can be imagined, many other important production jet fighters built during the 1940s and early 1950s that space does not allow to be included in lengthy detail. Among these must be included the US Navy's Ryan FR-1

Below: The high performing but simple Mikoyan-Gurevich MiG-15 was built in thousands for the Soviet forces and those of many other nations. Poland was one of the countries that undertook license production, the LiM-2 illustrated representing a Polish MiG-15*bis*.

Right: The first production version of the USAF's well-equipped North American Sabre fighter was the F-86A, blooded against the MiG-15 in the skies over Korea during the early 1950s.

Below right: The de Havilland Vampire F.Mk 1 was the RAF's first single-engined jet fighter, entering service in 1946.

Above: Republic F-84G Thunderjet in Turkish service.

Fireball, 66 of which were built, each with a nose-mounted Wright radial engine for cruising flight and a General Electric J31 turbojet in the tail end to attain dash speed. One made the first-ever landings by a jet-powered aircraft on an aircraft carrier, on 6 November 1945, following failure of the nose engine while making a landing approach to USS *Wake Island*. The Soviet Mikoyan-Gurevich MiG-9, powered by two Soviet-produced developments of the German BMW 003A engine, and the Yakovlev Yak-15, were that nation's first twin-engined and single-engined jet fighters in service respectively, both

Below: From 1954 to 1956 the Swedish Flygvapnet received its last examples of the Saab J 29 Tunnan fighter, as J 29Fs, the engine afterburner fitted to this version virtually doubling the rate of climb and improving the service ceiling.

of which had first flown in prototype form on 24 April 1946. A McDonnell FH-1 Phantom, a straight-winged single-seater, was the first US Navy pure jet fighter to land on an aircraft carrier, on 21 July 1946, while the USAF's Republic F-84G Thunderjet was that service's first fighter-bomber capable of delivering an atomic bomb onto target. In Europe, the first indigenous French jet fighter was the Dassault Ouragan, first flown on 29 February 1949, while Sweden boasted Europe's first jet with fully swept wings with its Saab-29 Tunnan, the first production examples of which entered service with the Flygvapnet in 1951 as day fighters.

As fighters were the first aircraft type to apply the new technology of turbojet power, it is correct that they be given the greatest part of this scene-setting chapter. But even during the war years of 1939–45 jet bombers and

reconnaissance aircraft had appeared, and the first steps had been taken to ensure the rapid postwar establishment of airliners with gas turbine engines on the world's most important air routes.

As early as 1940 the German RLM (aviation ministry) had planned a twin-jet high-speed reconnaissance aircraft, this in the year before Britain's first jet aircraft for experimental use even flew as the Gloster E.28/39. To be based around either the Junkers Jumo 109-004 or BMW 109-003, from this original specification germinated the Arado Ar 234 Blitz (Lightning). Unsophisticated in configuration, although with many very important innovations which included a pressurized cockpit for the single pilot (who was expected to occupy an ejection seat), the Ar 234 carried the engines in nacelles beneath the high-mounted wings. The pilot's cockpit was heavily glazed and formed the nose of the circular-section, semi-monocoque, stressed-skin fuselage.

Problems obtaining turbojet engines resulted in the first of the seven prototypes not flying until 15 June 1943, but then with great success. The original concept of using a jettisonable wheeled trolley for take off and a retractable skid undercarriage for landing proved unworkable and before long a nose-wheel gear had been designed. Because of this and other modifications, the planned 'A' production series was abandoned in favor of the Ar 234B. Production lines were established at Alt Lönnewitz.

The first of three Ar 234B prototypes flew on 19 March 1944 and on 8 June the first of twenty preproduction Ar 234B-0s took to the air. The Ar 234B-0s were completed without pressurized cabins or ejection seats and each could carry two reconnaissance cameras of various types. Of the 20, 13 were delivered to the flight-proving center at Rechlin. By this time, however, two of the original prototypes had undertaken the first operational missions by jet reconnaissance aircraft. Having been delivered to the evaluation unit 1 Staffel/Versuchsverband Ob d L at Juvincourt, less than two weeks after the arrival there of Me 262s belonging to KG 51 Kommando Schenck, the first mission was flown on 20 July 1944. Interestingly, this was the day Britain had completed deployment of its anti-aircraft guns around the English coast to counter German V-1 flying-bombs, but these were not to trouble the Arados.

Ar 234B-0s subsequently joined the unit but, with the availability of full-production Ar 234B-1 reconnaissance aircraft, the first operational unit proper was formed as Sonderkommando Götz. Two further units were formed soon after but in January 1945 these gave way to three new squadrons stationed in Denmark and at Rheine.

Historians record that the final German air mission over Britain of the

Second World War was flown from Norway by an Ar 234B reconnaissance aircraft of KG 76, on 10 April 1945. In general, reconnaissance sorties by Arado jets had been little troubled by defending RAF fighters, due mainly to their high speed and operating altitude of approximately 9000m (29,500ft). But KG 76 (Kampfgeschwader 76) is best remembered for operating the first ever purpose-built jet bombers.

The Arado Ar 234B-2 had been evolved to supersede the B-1 and was far more versatile. Featuring two rear-firing 20mm MG 151 cannon (with 200 rounds of ammunition per gun), a braking parachute and a Patin PDS three-axis autopilot to free the pilot to use the Lotfe 7K bombsight, it could be used for photographic reconnaissance, light bombing and pathfinding roles. Maximum speed was an impressive 742km/h (461mph) at 6000m (19,680ft) clean, although while carrying a 1000kg bombload speed was reduced to 645km/h (400mph). Like earlier *Blitz*, RATOG (rocket assisted take-off gear) was available, allowing shorter take-off distances or the carriage of a 1500kg warload.

The first Ar 234B-2 bombers were sent to KG 76 in October 1944, pilots receiving their initial jet training on two-seat Messerschmitt Me 262B-1a conversion aircraft belonging to IV(Erg)/KG 51. Blooding of KG 76's jet bombers came during the Allied Ardennes offensive, which lasted two months from 16 December 1944, at this time the first operational Gruppe of KG 76 operating from Rheine and Achmer. Other Gruppes of KG 76 became operational before fuel shortages prevented possible effective operations. However, the Arado jet bomber, in the company of Me 262 fighter-bombers, will always be remembered for its attacks during the Allied crossing of the Rhine. It is believed that fewer than 250 *Blitz* were ever completed for operational service in the war.

Below: The world's first jet-powered reconnaissance-bomber was the German Arado Ar 234 *Blitz*, a captured Ar 234B seen here in Allied markings.

In the strictest sense, the very first British and US jet-powered bombers were conventional piston-engined bombers modified to test single jet units in their tails. In this configuration Britain flew an Avro Lancaster and Vickers Wellington; in America the Douglas XA-26F Invader was created by the installation of a General Electric I-16 in the tail, by the deletion of the rear gun turret. The XA-26F differed from the British types, however, in being intended as an operational aircraft in production form and not merely engine testbed aircraft. The XA-26F first flew on 26 June 1946 and was therefore too late for the war.

Britain's first jet bomber intended for operational deployment was the English Electric Canberra, first flown in prototype form as the A.1 on 13 May 1949. No 101 Squadron was the first of the RAF's operational jet bomber units, receiving Canberra B.Mk 2s as Avro Lincoln replacements in May 1951. The first of many versions of the Canberra for various duties with the RAF and many other nations, the B.Mk 2 was a three-seater powered by two Rolls-Royce Avon turbojets carried Meteor-

Below left: The A-26F version of the Douglas Invader had been intended for production, with a tail installed I-16 turbojet engine supplementing the usual radial engines.

Right: The English Electric A.1, prototype of Britain's first ever jet bomber.

Below: After the English Electric Canberra B.Mk 2 came the B.Mk 6, remembered as the first RAF jet bomber to be used in anger when operated against anti-government forces in Malaya.

fashion in the wings. Such was the potential of the Canberra that the type was selected for service with the USAF as a night intruder, produced under license as the Martin B-57. Two Canberra B.Mk 2s flown to the USA to help Martin set up production actually made the first ever transatlantic flights by turbojet-powered aircraft without refueling, on 21 February 1951.

The adoption of the Canberra by the USAF did not indicate a lack of progress in the field of jet bombers by US aircraft manufacturers. Far from it. The first American purpose-designed jet bomber had been the Douglas XB-43 Mixmaster, ordered as a prototype in early 1944. The first of two examples took to the air for its first flight on 17 May 1946. Powered by two 1700kg (3750lb) st General Electric TG-180 turbojets carried in the rear fuselage, the XB-43 managed an impressive 828km/h (515mph) but was not ordered into production.

In 1947 the USAF's new Strategic Air Command began to receive early examples of the Boeing B-50 and Convair B-36s. These heavy bombers were

its last with piston engines. The same year five prototype jet bombers flew for the first time. Of these, the North American B-45 Tornado, first flown in prototype form on 17 March 1947, became the USAF's first operational jet bomber, first going to the 47th Bombardment Group in late 1948. Powered by four J35 turbojets, the General Electric TG-180 in production form, subsequently managed by Allison in prototype and initial production forms, maximum speed was raised from just over 800km/h (500mph) with these engines to 932km/h (579mph) with General Electric J47 turbojets selected for later versions.

The most important early US jet bomber, and the USAF's first six-jet production bomber, was the Boeing B-47 Stratojet. Powered by J47s in production form, take-off performance was boosted by JATO rocket motors installed in the fuselage. First flown in prototype form on 17 December 1947, the Stratojet served for many years and was produced in large numbers. Indeed, no fewer than 1590 examples of the main variant, the B-47E, were com-

pleted, a figure including RB-47E day and night photographic reconnaissance variants. It was not until 1969 that the last of the USAF's B-47s were retired, although they had been serving only as weather reconnaissance aircraft.

The first Soviet jet bomber to fly was the Ilyushin Il-22, on 24 July 1947. Powered by four underwing TR-1 engines, it was rejected for production. However, Ilyushin's later Il-28 was to prove one of the finest early jet bombers to serve anywhere in the world. The first of three Il-28 prototypes made its maiden flight on 8 August 1948 on the power of two RD-45 (Soviet built Rolls-Royce Nene development) engines, demonstrating subsequently a speed of 833km/h (517mph). However, this was its non-equipped speed. With armament and operational equipment installed the speed fell by nearly 80km/h (50mph). Eventually, two VK-1 engines produced by Klimov became standard on production Il-28s, and these (known to NATO under the reporting name *Beagle*) attained speeds of up to 902km/h (560mph).

While the Il-28 was the Soviet air force's first jet bomber, the first for

Soviet Naval Aviation was the Tupolev Tu-14. Later known to NATO as *Bosun*, most were powered by two VK-1 engines and were operated with a main armament of bombs or torpedoes. However, Tu-14s were produced in much smaller number than the Il-28, were less successful and were out of service by the early 1960s. The type also failed to win international status, remaining Soviet operated only. The fact that the Il-28 remains in operational use outside the Soviet Union in the 1980s gives some indication of its international acceptance, which has been on a level with the British Canberra. As to which of the two Soviet bombers was the first in operational service, it is considered that the Il-28 pipped the Tu-14, not least because it completed its acceptance trials before the Tu-14 in 1949 and an impressive force of twenty-five Il-28s took part in the 1950 May Day flypast.

The bombers mentioned in the previous paragraphs, and the fighters before, represent just the first few of many such aircraft put into service prior to what can be termed *Modern Jet Aircraft*. But no scene-setting chapter on the beginnings of jet aircraft operation would be complete without reference to the first ever jet airliners and military transports.

On 4 December 1942 Liberator bombers carried out the first USAAF attack on Italy of the war. On the 22nd of the same month USAAF Liberators made the first major air raid on a Japanese operated air station in the Central Pacific, while on the 24th Australian forces contributed to the recapture of the Buna airstrip in New Guinea. Meanwhile, on the night of 20–21 December, RAF Mosquito bombers carrying Oboe radar had been used for the first time on a night pathfinder mission. It was in this wartime atmosphere, with no prospect of an Allied invasion of Europe to mark the final phase of the world war, that the British government set up the so-called Brabazon Committee. Under the chairmanship of Lord Brabazon of Tara, its role was to formulate recommendations relating to new civil transport aircraft that would be required after the end of hostilities.

A number of the aircraft evolved from the Committee's recommendations resulted in piston-engined air-

liners, including the giant and unsuccessful eight-engined Bristol Type 167 Brabazon Mk 1 London-New York airliner and the small twin-engined de Havilland DH 104 Dove. However, another recommendation matured into the de Havilland DH 106 Comet 1, the world's first turbojet-powered airliner. But while the Comet was the first jet airliner, it was not the first with gas-turbine engines to be operated on scheduled airline services.

Back in May 1944, Rolls-Royce had begun work on an adaption of its Derwent engine to drive a propeller. The resulting turboprop engine was known as the Trent. Two such units were flight tested on a Meteor fighter-type airframe, flown initially on 20 September 1945. This marked the first

Above: The USAF's first operational jet bomber was the four-engined North American B-45A Tornado, first going to the 47th Bombardment Group in 1948.

Below: Marking a new era for the USAF, the Boeing B-47 Stratojet prototype stands proud alongside one of that service's last piston-engined bombers, the Boeing B-50.

24

Below: One of a few Ilyushin Il-28
Beagle light jet bombers in service with
the Egyptian Air Force.

Left: Less successful than the Il-28 was
Soviet Naval Aviation's Tu-14 *Bosun*.

flight of a turboprop engine and a turboprop-powered aircraft. The Trent was basically a research engine, the lessons learned going into the design of the Rolls-Royce Dart. This engine was the first specifically designed turboprop engine to fly, when in October 1947 it was tested in the nose of an Avro Lancaster.

Incredibly, the Rolls-Royce Dart, initially rated at 990shp, remains in production and under development in the 1980s. The latest versions, giving outputs of more than 2000shp, power British and overseas aircraft, including the British Aerospace HS 748 passenger and freight transport. But, in its early form, the Dart was the chosen power plant for the world's first gas turbine-powered aircraft to fly, the British Vickers Viscount.

The Viscount had been conceived in 1945 as a 24-passenger airliner to use the Dart engine then under development at Rolls-Royce. By the time the engine had reached a practical stage in its development, it had become clear that its output was going to be about 25% up on the original estimate. With such power available from its four

engines, the decision was made to construct the prototype Viscount as a 32-seat airliner. On 16 July 1948 Viscount *G-AHRF* made its maiden flight at Wisley in Surrey. On 28 July 1950 it received the first certificate of airworthiness for a turbine-powered airliner.

Left: This ex-BEA Vickers V.806 Viscount, once in commercial use with Cambrian, represented a stretched version of the Type 700 (for 65 passengers).

Below left: Lockheed entered the turboprop-powered commercial airliner business with its L.188 Electra.

Below: One of Air New Zealand's Fokker F.27 Friendship Mk 500s. This version has the longest fuselage of any F.27, accommodating 52 passengers.

liner and on the following day BEA introduced it experimentally on its London-Paris service, so recording the world's first scheduled service by a gas turbine-powered airliner. Such was its success and high degree of passenger comfort that on 3 August BEA ordered twenty production Type 701 Viscounts, the first of many orders for Viscounts in several variants from airlines around the world. Other noteworthy dates are 15 August, when BEA introduced the prototype on its London-Edinburgh route, so establishing the first domestic service with a gas turbine-powered airliner; 18 April, when the same company inaugurated its first sustained service with the Viscount, between London and Nicosia; and 3 June 1954, when Vickers got into the important US market with the announcement of Viscounts ordered by Capital Airlines.

Even before the Viscount prototype had flown, BOAC had issued a requirement for a medium-range turboprop-powered airliner to serve Empire routes. To this was developed the Bristol Type 175 Britannia, a sixty- to ninety-passenger airliner adopting four Bristol Proteus turboprop engines. Because of the very high output rating of the Proteus engine, the same power plant had been selected also for the two largest aircraft then under construction in Britain, the Mk 2 version of the huge Brabazon airliner and the giant Saunders-Roe Princess ten-engined flying-boat. The former, in the event, was never finished, and the 66.9m (219ft 6in)-span 105- to 220-seat Princess remained a prototype following BOAC's decision to give up flying-boats for its long-haul ocean routes.

The first of two Britannia prototypes (*G-ALBO*) flew for the first time on 16 August 1952 and fifteen examples of the Britannia 102, the first production version, were ordered by BOAC. Britannias entered commercial service on 1 February 1957 as that airline's first turboprop-powered airliners, on its London-Johannesburg route. Longer fuselage versions followed for BOAC and overseas airlines, plus military derivatives.

In America, General Electric had produced that nation's first indigenous turboprop engine as the TG-100A, completed and initially tested in 1943 and first flight tested on an experimental Consolidated Vultee XP-81 fighter on 21 December 1945. The XP-81 had been conceived as a single-seat long-range escort fighter for the Pacific theater of war, powered by the turboprop (military designated XT31) in the fuselage nose and an Allison J33 turbojet in the tail. Poor power output from the XT31, combined with the fact that hostilities with Japan had by then ended, brought an end to the fighter project.

Another US pioneering company of the turboprop was Allison, a Division of General Motors Corporation. This company developed the XT38, which demonstrated an output of 3600shp under test. One aircraft that flew the XT38 was the McDonnell XF-88B, a research fighter used solely to investigate the design of supersonic propellers that was first flown in April 1953. However, Allison had, much earlier, developed its XT40 for the US Navy. This consisted of two XT38 axial-flow power sections coupled to drive two contra-rotating three-blade propellers via reduction gear. Flight tested on various aircraft in the early 1950s, including experimental tail-sitting VTOL fighters in YT40 preproduction form, the engine was the power plant for the US Navy's only turboprop-powered flying-boat to enter service, the Convair R3Y Tradewind freight and personnel transport and flight refueling tanker.

Meanwhile, in 1954 Allison had flight tested a much-improved turboprop engine as the T56, evolved from the T38 and first installed experimentally in the nose of a Boeing B-17 Flying Fortress. Later two Convair YC-131Cs, military examples of the Convair-Liner 340 airliner, were tested with YT56 engines by the 1700th Test Squadron of MATS, USAF, the first flying on 29 June 1954.

The initial production version of the Allison engine was the T56-A-1. This was selected by the Lockheed Aircraft Corporation for its pioneering work on turboprop transports, both for military and commercial use. But it should not be forgotten that in the mid-1950s piston-engined airliners were still very much in vogue: Douglas had only recently seen its DC-7 into service and Lockheed itself had still to fly its ultimate variant of the Constellation, the L-1649A Starliner (first flown in October 1956). However, on 23 August 1954 Lockheed flew the first prototype of a new medium assault transport for the USAF, designated YC-130. Powered by four 3750eshp T56-A-1 engines, the first of many production versions (that continue to be available today) was the C-130A.

For the medium-range commercial airliner market, Lockheed developed its L.188 Electra, powered by the civil version of the T56 known as the Allison 501. American Airlines ordered no fewer than 35 'off the drawing board' in 1955 and the first Electra flew on 6 December 1957. Eastern Air Lines and American Airlines put the 66-seat version into service in January 1959.

In late 1955 the Netherlands gained an early foothold in the medium-size and medium-range airliner market with the appearance of the Fokker F.27 Friendship, a 28-passenger aircraft powered by two Rolls-Royce Dart engines. Also produced for some time in the USA as the Fairchild F-27 and FH-227, the first Friendship deliveries took place in November 1958. The Friendship today still enjoys great success in commercial and military variants.

Although not the first nation to use turboprop power, it can be said that the Soviet Union has done more to further its widespread use over the years than any other. This simple fact centers upon the production of the Kuznetsov NK-12M, today the most powerful turboprop engine in the world (in its NK-12MV version rated at 14,795ehp) but first developed by a team of engineers led by Nikolai Kuznetsov and including Germans. This, of course, was not the first Soviet turboprop engine developed but was particularly important for two reasons. Firstly, it enabled Tupolev to develop the huge Tu-95 *Bear* very long range bomber, providing not only sufficient power for the large airframe but the fuel economy necessary for long range. Secondly, by adopting the Tu-95's wings and engines, tail unit and other components, Tupolev was able to construct the Tu-114 Rossiya, completed in 1957 as the world's largest and heaviest commercial airliner.

The Tu-95 bomber, and its maritime counterpart the Tu-142, remain in service in strategic roles today, their importance being shown by continued limited production to make good normal attrition. However the Tu-114, which in June 1959 demonstrated its ability to fly non-stop from Moscow to New York in a little over eleven hours, is not to be seen in use. In its original form it proved capable of accommodating a staggering 220 passengers. Production included the later Tu-114D version with a shorter and slimmer fuselage, to enable fewer passengers and/or mail/freight to be transported over longer ranges. The Tu-114 today forms the basis of the Tu-126 *Moss*, the Soviet military AWACS (airborne warning and control system) aircraft which features a large rotodome above the fuselage.

Precursor of today's range of Antonov military and civil transports was the An-8, first seen in 1956 and powered by two Kuznetsov NK-6TV-2 turboprop engines. A larger four-turboprop development of the An-8 was the An-10, conceived as an 84-passenger airliner using Kuznetsov NK-4 turboprops. It is sometimes recorded that for production models, which entered Aeroflot from 1959, NK-4s were changed for Ivchenko AI-20s. This is indeed correct, although often forgotten is that the AI-20 was no more than the refined NK-4 in production form.

While the Vickers Viscount had started the ball rolling for turboprop transports, to the majority of the world's aircraft manufacturers the turbojet engine appeared more attractive because of potential higher speeds. Rapid postwar development of turbojets produced a range that were less thirsty for fuel than the first-generation engines and so could offer reasonable range in addition to higher speeds. One aircraft manufacturing company that produced a design that originally specified turboprops but was later modified to take turbojets was Boeing, which had proposed a new heavy bomber using gas turbine engines even before the USAAF/USAF began receiving its last newly built piston-engined bombers.

Boeing's proposal was for a large straight-winged bomber adopting no fewer than six turboprop engines of a type then under development as the Wright XT-35. This design was later refined to include sweptback wings, subsequently going through the further process of having the turboprop engines replaced by eight very new Pratt & Whitney J57 turbojets. In this form the prototype Boeing B-52 Stratofortress strategic bomber was constructed, making its first flight on 15 April 1952. Boeing was also to develop and produce the world's first turbojet-powered airliner of a size that could be called 'jumbo jet', not the Model 747 in this case but the Model 707, although it was to Britain that went the prestige of flying the very first turbojet-powered airliner.

The de Havilland DH 106 Comet was produced to fulfil one of the recommendations of the wartime Brabazon Committee. For its time it was as technically advanced as was Concorde several generations later, featuring the first use of turbojet engines on a large passenger aircraft, moderately sweptback wings and pressurized cabins, and was designed to include in its equipment an electronic automatic pilot. Intended to operate over Commonwealth trunk routes in the hands of BOAC, as well as international services of a more general nature, the Comet became de Havilland's main postwar commercial project, its development starting in 1947.

Such were the expectations of the Comet that, even before the prototype had made its maiden flight, work was initiated on two production Comet 1s for the Ministry of Supply and fourteen for BOAC. The prototype Comet *G-ALVG* flew for the first time at Hatfield, Hertfordshire, on 27 July 1949, so recording the historically important first flight of a turbojet-powered airliner. Its potential was amply demonstrated on 25 October that year when a Comet was flown from London to Tripoli and back in a single day, further endorsed by the setting of a new world point-to-point record between London and Cairo on 24 April 1950 during tropical trials.

The next major milestone in the Comet's career came on 22 January 1952, when it received the first Certificate of Airworthiness given to a turbo-jet-powered airliner. BOAC began receiving Comet 1s the following month and on 2 May 1952 the airline inaugurated the world's first scheduled jet airliner service, covering the London-Johannesburg route in a little over $23\frac{1}{2}$ hours. Within two months proving flights to Tokyo had started, followed in August by a weekly service to Colombo. Using the Comet on a weekly

Below: The definitive version of the de Havilland Comet was the 4C, two of which were operated by Sudan Airways.

Forty-four passengers and longer stage lengths were introduced with the Comet 1A and all seemed set for an impressive future. In February 1953 Union Aéromaritime de Transport (UAT) became the first foreign operator of the Comet and others quickly followed. But, on the first anniversary of the inauguration of Comet services, a BOAC Comet 1 suffered structural failure and crashed near Calcutta with heavy loss of life.

This tragic accident was not to prevent further acceptance of the Comet internationally, and in August Air France became a new operator. The

caused metal fatigue to the fuselage structure, resulting in an explosive decompression.

Naturally, faith in the Comet faltered and Comet 2s ordered for BOAC were strengthened and some became military aircraft with the RAF. The redesigned and lengthened Comet 3 remained a prototype but the Comet 4 returned the airliner into commercial service. In 1957 BOAC ordered 19 examples of the Comet 4, a 60- to 81-passenger airliner with a new longer fuselage, increased engine power from its Avon 524 turbojets, greater fuel capacity and much improved range. The first Comet 4 made

service from April 1953, the normal flying time to Tokyo was reduced from 86 hours to just over 33 hours.

The Comet 1, which had reached BOAC a full six months ahead of schedule, was a 36-passenger airliner powered by four 2291kg (5050lb)st de Havilland Ghost 50 turbojet engines buried within the wing roots. Hinged panels in the underwing surfaces exposed the installations for servicing on the ground. With a full payload and fuel reserves, the Comet 1 was best suited to stage lengths of about 2414km (1500 miles). Cruising speed was about 788km/h (490mph), while the high cruising altitude that could be attained ensured maximum passenger comfort.

same day of August, the 27th, de Havilland introduced the Comet 2 option, featuring a slightly lengthened fuselage, more powerful Rolls-Royce Avon engines and much improved stage lengths. However, fortunes were about to change. On 10 January 1954 a BOAC Comet 1 broke up in the air while serving a route to London from the Far East, falling into the Mediterranean with all on board lost. On 8 April another BOAC Comet 1 broke up, this time over Naples, again with all passengers and crew lost. Now there was little choice but to withdraw the Comet from service pending investigations. These subsequently revealed that the extensive use of pressurization had

its maiden flight on 27 April 1958. Deliveries to BOAC began in September and on 4 October BOAC began the first jet airliner services across the North Atlantic, between London and New York. Thereafter BOAC began extensive use of Comets over its international network and others were delivered to foreign airlines. From the Comet 4 were developed the lengthened Comet 4B and 4C, the former having a reduced wing span for higher speeds and both accommodating 101 passengers. Of the 112 Comets of all versions built, 74 were of the Comet 4 series. The last of these, operated by Dan-Air, were withdrawn only a few years ago. However, the basic Comet configura-

tion lives on in the RAF's Nimrod maritime patrol aircraft.

Back in 1944 Boeing flew the prototype of its Model 367 which, in later production form, became a standard cargo and troop transport and a flight refueling tanker with the USAF under various C-97 Stratofreighter designations. Boeing's last piston-engined type to enter production, a civil airliner variant of the same aircraft followed as the Model 377 Stratocruiser, which introduced a hitherto unknown standard of luxury for passengers.

When Boeing made the decision to develop a turbojet transport to replace the USAF's C-97 series, it deliberately adopted the model number 367-80 to give the impression that its new aircraft was just a developed Stratofreighter. Nothing could have been further from the truth. Using four turbojet engines of the type selected for its B-52 bomber, though known as Pratt & Whitney JT3s in civil form, the prototype was rolled-out at the company's Renton plant in mid-1954 and flew for the first time on 15 July 1954. Often referred to simply as 'Dash-Eighty', it was America's first turbojet-powered transport to fly.

A 'jumbo jet' of its period, the Model 367-80 had a wing span of 39.52m (129ft 8in), a length of 38.95m (127ft 10in) and a maximum take-off weight of a staggering 86,182kg (190,000lb). Compared even to Britain's contemporary Comet, which had a wing span, length and maximum take-off weight of 35.05m (115ft), 28.35m (93ft) and 47,627kg (105,000lb) respectively, the US aircraft was gargantuan. From June 1957 many hundreds of production aircraft entered USAF service as KC-135 Stratotankers, C-135 Stratolifters and in other forms for a variety of specialist duties.

Almost exactly a year after the Model 367-80 had first flown, Boeing was given permission to construct commercial airliner variants concurrently with production of military transports. Considering the Model 367-80 had been conceived and built as a private venture and that it was by then to be the precursor of military transports and probably very large numbers of commercial airliners, Boeing must have considered the financial gamble one of its greatest achievements. Indeed, although then unknown to the company, the jetliner was to remain in production for a quarter of a century.

The initial production version of the airliner was company designated Model 707-120. Intended for US domestic operation but with sufficient range for overocean use, the first customer, Pan American World Airways, put it into transatlantic service between New

Above: Meeting of the old and the new: the prototype Boeing 707 jetliner was parked alongside a replica of a 1912 Curtiss biplane for a publicity photograph.

York and Paris from 28 October 1958. This was just a little over three weeks after Britain had opened transatlantic jetliner services.

The Model 707-120 operated on four JT3C-6 turbojet engines installed in pods beneath the sweptback wings and had accommodation for an impressive 181 passengers. More than any other early jet airliner, the Model 707 was to introduce to the masses fast, reliable and safe jet air travel.

Many versions of the Model 707 followed, including the Model 707-120B with turbofan engines, the long-range Model 707-320 Intercontinental and the Model 707-320C Convertible, the latter offering accommodation for up to 219 passengers or all cargo or a mix of passengers and cargo. A total of well over 900 Model 707s and related Model 720s were completed before production ended, although the Model 707 still forms the basis of the military E-3 Sentry AWACS aircraft, under construction for the USAF, NATO and Saudi Arabia. Maximum cruising speed and range of the Model 707-120 were quoted as 919km/h (571mph) and 5177km (3217 miles) respectively.

31

France was the third nation to fly a turbojet-powered airliner, although this had to rely for its power on Rolls-Royce Avon engines. The Caravelle was also the world's first rear-engined jetliner, designed by the Société Nationale de Constructions Aéronautiques du Sud-Est (SNCASE) and flown for the first time on 27 May 1955. The first production SE 210 Caravelle appeared almost exactly three years later and in May 1959 Air France and SAS put the airliner into service.

By the close of production, in 1972, more than 282 Caravelles had been completed. Those remaining in service today are examples of the Caravelle VIR, each powered by two Avon 533R engines. Seating 99 passengers, this version cruises at 845km/h (525mph) and has a normal range of about 2300km (1430 miles). Interestingly, on 28 December 1955, when Air France announced its order for 24 Caravelles, it also announced its intended procurement of ten Boeing Model 707s, indicating the importance of the US jetliner even to France's national carrier. Air France, therefore, received examples of all three of the world's first turbojet airliners.

Less than three weeks was to elapse between the prototype Caravelle taking off and the initial flight of the first Soviet turbojet-powered airliner, the Tupolev Tu-104. Its design and construction had been meteoric, begun in 1953 but aided considerably by the use of similar wings and engine installations, tail unit, undercarriage and other component parts to those of the newly developed Tu-16 twin-jet strategic bomber. It was therefore the case that both the Tupolev Tu-114 turboprop airliner and the Tu-104 were based on bomber designs.

Carrying just 50 passengers, the early production Tu-104 nevertheless revolutionized Aeroflot services on selected routes, beginning with the airline's Moscow, Omsk and Irkutsk service on 15 September 1956, exactly 15 months after the airliner's first flight. The Tu-104 was followed by the more powerful Tu-104A, a 70-passenger version that achieved some export success. Other versions were built, including a 115-passenger variant but few, if any, remain in use today. Tu-104s were also used in military guise, its varied duties including cosmonaut training. From the 800km/h (497mph) Tu-104 was evolved the similar but four-jet Tu-110, first shown at Vnukovo Airport in Moscow in July 1957 but which did not achieve production status, and the similar but smaller short-range twin-jet Tu-124, which first flew as a 44-passenger airliner in mid-1960. Perhaps the most significant aspect of Tupolev's initial jet airliner efforts was that its Tu-104 became only the world's second jetliner in commercial service, pre-empting the US and French types that appeared before the Tu-104 in prototype form.

The huge Tu-114, mentioned previously, had not been the first Soviet airliner to fly with turboprop engines and was by no means the most important early type. Far more significant was the Il-18, Ilyushin's follow-up to its radial-engined Il-14. The prototype Il-18 took to the air for the first time on 4 July 1957 and by 1959 was in Aeroflot service.

The Il-18 reflected similar thinking that had produced the Lockheed Electra in the USA, although the Soviet airliner was designed and built as a larger aircraft. All three civil production versions were fitted with Ivchenko AI-20 turboprop engines of various models and accommodation ranged from 65 to 122 passengers. Approximately 560 Il-18 airliners were completed for Aeroflot and foreign airlines, of which nearly half are still in use. Some, however, have more recently been stripped for freighting work. Such was the importance of the Il-18 to Aeroflot in the years following its entry into service that over a period of two decades the airliner was responsible for the carriage of an estimated 235 million passengers. Maximum speed of refined versions is 675km/h (420mph), while range is thought to be about 3700km (2299 miles). The Il-18 also ranks as one of the most important

Below: The SE 210 Caravelle 12, the final 'stretched' version of the Caravelle, offering accommodation for up to 139 passengers.

Above right: Refueling a Tupolev Tu-104B, the longest variant of the Tu-104 with seats for 100 passengers.

Below right: One of the major operators of the Ilyushin Il-18 is CAAC. This example is seen at Beijing.

Soviet airliners in terms of export success.

Early gas turbine-powered aircraft, whether military or commercial using the simple turbojet or more economical turboprop, revolutionized warfare and air travel to a similar extent. The success of these served to fuel the quest for faster, larger or more specialized aircraft, powered by refined variants of existing engines or newly developed power plants. The first supersonic fighters appeared in the early 1950s, followed soon after by the first super-

sonic bombers, although the world had to wait until 1968 for the first supersonic airliner.

There is some controversy on both sides of the Atlantic as to whether the term jet aircraft encompasses all aircraft with gas turbine engines or whether the term relates only to those aircraft with turbojet and turbofan engines that generate actual jet thrust. With a turboprop (and similarly the turboshaft for helicopters) the majority of the power generated by the engine goes directly into turning the propeller

and therefore the aircraft's forward motion is not the direct result of a high-velocity gas jet discharged through a nozzle. Therefore, while the term propjet is common in the USA for turboprop, only those aircraft fitted with turbojet or turbofan engines are included in the following chapters. This does not invalidate the detailing of turboprop-powered aircraft earlier in this first chapter, as it is deemed important that a proper understanding of the relationship between both forms of early gas turbine-powered aircraft is established.

Substantial numbers of some of the early jet aircraft mentioned previously, and others that followed, remain in use today. But, for obvious reasons, they cannot be termed *Modern Jet Aircraft* and so have no place in the following chapters. As a principle had to be established to distinguish the modern types, it is reasonable that only those civil and military aircraft that have been in production in the last few years should be included. This principle has, however, the interesting effect of ensuring the inclusion of several aircraft that first appeared three decades or more ago and have enjoyed long production runs in their countries of origin or abroad. There have to be, nonetheless, one or more exceptions to this guideline, made necessary to enable inclusion of aircraft like the USAF's Boeing B-52 Stratofortress, which today remains that service's and NATO's only long-range heavy strategic bomber.

CHAPTER TWO

A CASE FOR CAUTIOUS OPTIMISM

BOEING, LOCKHEED & McDONNELL

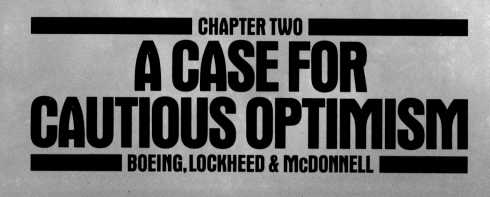

The United States of America is the world's leading manufacturer of commercial transport aircraft and a large-scale producer of military aircraft. Production of military aircraft for the US armed services depends partly on the political willingness of government to allocate the necessary funds for their purchase and this has not always proven easy to secure. Conversely, the market place has been the barometer for airliner sales and production, interspersed with forced purchases due to the requirement to meet new operating standards or other factors.

In the late 1970s it was generally agreed that the future looked healthy for world commercial aviation. There appeared little risk in airlines planning to increase or modernize their fleets at very high cost and the manufacturers were willing to ride the tide. Boeing, the world's most important producer of commercial aircraft, went a stage further by initiating production of a new family of large airliners, although only after the customary initial orders had been secured. The world recession that followed so unexpectedly caught manufacturers and operators by surprise, forcing some airlines to rethink purchases and others to go out of

One of several Boeing Model 707-320s operated by Bangladesh Biman.

business, while many major manufacturers were suddenly starved of orders for their largest and costliest aircraft. Now that the world is gradually reviving from the recession, the aircraft business is leaner and more efficient but also less willing to gamble huge sums of money on aircraft development or purchase in such a potentially volatile market.

Since the end of the Second World War US airliners have dominated the world air transport scene, the nation's earliest jet airliners proving generally more practical for international use than those built in other countries that preceded them. The very first US jetliner, the Boeing 707, was only discontinued in commercial form in 1982, when the final Model 707-320C was delivered to Morocco. This version had been the sole available 707 variant for some years prior to this delivery and represented the most versatile. In passenger airliner form it accommodates up to 219 passengers, its easily changeable interior layout allowing also for a smaller number of passengers to be carried with cargo, or it can be flown in all-cargo form.

By 1983 the Model 707-320C had completed two decades of service. It shares having the largest 707 airframe with the slightly earlier Model 707-320B airliner and the VC-137C – the latter being the -320B operated by the USAF as the *Air Force One* Presidential transport – with a wing span and length of 43.41m (142ft 5in) and 46.61m (152ft 11in) respectively, although weighing the most at a gross weight of 151,315kg (333,600lb). Its four Pratt & Whitney JT3D-7 turbofan engines provide a cruising speed of 973km/h (605mph) and a range with 147 passengers of 9265km (5755 miles).

In 1983 production of the Model 707 airframe continued, but for a very different purpose. Since 1978 the USAF has been deploying small numbers of the Boeing E-3 Sentry, an AWACS (Airborne Warning And Control System) aircraft based on the Model 707. Basically, the Sentry is an airborne radar station and communications aircraft, packed with the most sophisticated avionics and carrying a Westinghouse radar in a circular slow-turning rotodome above the fuselage. Powered by four Pratt & Whitney TF33-PW-100

Above: The Boeing Model 707 airframe forms the basis of the E-3 Sentry AWACS aircraft, featuring a 9.14m (30ft) diameter rotodome supported on a pylon above the fuselage.

Right: The engine arrangement of the Boeing 727 is clearly shown by this airliner operated by Alaska Airlines.

or 100A turbofan engines, its role is to detect and track any type of enemy aircraft, RPV or tactical missile flying at low, medium or high altitude in all weathers and over all types of terrain. Some, including those E-3As now in use with NATO in Europe and initially based in West Germany, have the added capability of comprehensive maritime surveillance. In addition, the E-3 has the task of directing the deployment of friendly aircraft to assist in air defense (as for NORAD – the North American continent air defense system) and can assist tactical aircraft during strike missions. To date the USAF has received 34 E-3s and NATO is to deploy eighteen. The first of NATO's aircraft became operational in 1983. Five may also find their way to the Royal Saudi Air Force in 1985, although these will not have all the latest equipment of USAF/NATO aircraft.

The Model 707 airframe is also to form the basis of the E-6, an airborne communications aircraft intended for US service in the latter years of this decade to provide a communications link between command authorities and the Navy's ballistic submarines patrolling at sea. Each of the E-6s, of which fifteen are wanted, will be powered by CFM International CFM56 turbofan engines of very advanced type, as also currently being retrofitted to the USAF's fleet of KC-135A flight refueling tanker aircraft.

Boeing, having produced the first US jetliner which, by 1960, was established in airline service, announced its next jetliner as the Model 727. This was not intended as a replacement for the 707

and similar 720 but to expand the market. Not surprisingly, a number of Model 707 component parts found their way into the Model 727, including the upper fuselage, but to the layman similarities were not apparent. The new airliner was intended as a smaller transport, initially offering accommodation for only 131 passengers, and so was given just three rear-mounted turbofan engines and the necessary T-tail.

The first example of the Model 727 took off for its maiden flight on 9 February 1963 and commercial services with the airliner were inaugurated by Eastern Air Lines on the first day of February 1964. Since then the Model 727 in all its versions has proved to be the world's best-selling airliner, of which well over 1800 have been delivered to customers worldwide. The currently available versions are the

Advanced 727-200 and 727-200F freighter, the former accommodating 145-189 passengers and the windowless freighter carrying a payload (which includes the cargo handling system) of up to 28,620kg (63,102lb). Alternative models of the Pratt & Whitney JT8D turbofan engine are offered for these aircraft, allowing a cruising speed of 964km/h (599mph) and a range of up to 2487km (4003 miles) with a full load.

In 1983 Boeing announced that production of the Model 727 was to end in 1984, when the 1832nd example left the factory. This meant that by July 1983 only one Model 727 remained unsold. Shut down of the Model 727 production line gives some indication of Boeing's expectations for its latest airliners. Meanwhile, the company's smallest jetliner continues to be built and developed. This is the twin-turbofan and short-range Model 737, also used

Above: The smallest airliner of the Boeing range is the Model 737. The domestic operator Air Liberia purchased this Model 737-200C.

Inset: One of the more recent airlines to take up the Boeing 737 is LanChile, its 737-200 pictured with Mount Rainier tucked under its tail.

by the USAF as a military navigation trainer under the designation T-43A and by the Indonesian Air Force for maritime patrol and transport duties.

The first example of the Model 737 flew for the first time on 9 April 1967 and the type was initially offered in the 103-seat 737-100 form. The first order was placed by the German airline Lufthansa. Currently available from Boeing are the Advanced 737-200, a 115-130 passenger airliner powered by two underwing JT8D turbofans; the Advanced 737-200C convertible passenger and cargo derivative with an optional QC 'quick change' facility to speed the conversion of the aircraft's interior; an Executive Jet version of the Advanced 737-200 with a luxury interior for fewer passengers; and a higher weight version of the Model 737-200, intended to increase range by the addition of an extra fuel tank carried in the rear freight hold. By the late summer of 1983 Boeing had delivered 975 Model 737s to customers around the world. Cruising speed and typical range of the standard current model are 856km/h (532mph) and 3437km (2136 miles) respectively.

Proving that further development of a long established airliner can be very worthwhile, Boeing is currently working on the Model 737-300, intended for commercial service at the end of 1984. Based on the successful Advanced 737-200, it has a fuselage lengthened by several feet to increase the number of passengers that can be accommodated to a maximum of 149. The normal minimum number of passenger seats fitted will be 122. In addition, a very important change will be the adoption of two CFM International CFM56-3 turbofan engines in place of the standard JT8Ds, the new advanced engines offering improvements in both the amount of fuel burned and noise levels. However, the Model 737-300 has been developed to expand the 737 range and not to supersede existing models. The first customer for the Model 737-300 was USAir.

Even before the first Model 737 flew, Boeing had been hard at work preparing the design of a new airliner that was to be as revolutionary in concept as its Model 707 had been in the 1950s. This emerged as the Model 747, the world's first wide-bodied jetliner that overnight doubled the number of passengers that could be carried by a single aircraft. The first Model 747, with its now easily distinguishable upper deck hump, took off for its maiden flight on 9 February 1969. Fittingly, it was Pan American that introduced this gargantuan aircraft into service, making its first revenue flight over the New York-London route on 22 January 1970.

Dubbed 'Jumbo Jet' by the press, the aircraft in its earliest 747-100 form broke all records for airliners in size and weight. Wing span was an impressive 59.64m (195ft 8in), length 70.66m (231ft 10in) and weight 334,751kg (738,000lb). Accommodating 452 to 516 passengers, its four large Pratt & Whitney JT9D-7 series turbofan engines carried on pylons under the sweptback wings allowed a maximum speed of 958km/h (595mph). The range of 9136km (5677 miles) made the Model 747 the first Boeing jetliner with long-range from the outset.

This first variant, of which 167 were sold to operators around the world, is not among the versions currently offered for sale. The only -100 series Model 747 available is the Model 747-100B, introduced in 1979 with strengthened wings, fuselage and undercarriage and offering the options of Pratt & Whitney JT9D-7 series, General Electric CF6 or Rolls-Royce RB211-524 engines. However, sales for this version have been small.

Meanwhile, in 1971 deliveries started of the Model 747-200B, a heavier variant of the 747 with the longest range of any standard-fuselage model. Available with six engine model options within the types detailed above, it has an incredible possible maximum take-off weight of 377,840kg (833,000lb), making it the heaviest production aircraft in the world of either civil or military type. The Model 747-200B is also the most popular version of the 'Jumbo Jet', having accounted for more than one-third of the 600+ so far ordered.

Boeing also offers the basic airframe 747 in 747-200B Combi, 747-200C Convertible and 747-200F Freighter forms. The first of these to appear was the Freighter, in 1971. Based on the 747-200, it has no side windows but features a hinged nose door to allow straight-in loading of bulk cargo. A large fuselage side door is available to give access to the main deck. The underfloor cargo holds are served by side doors. The maximum payload of the Freighter depends on the engines fitted, but can be as high as 112,490kg (248,000lb). Range with a 90,720kg (200,000lb) payload at maximum take off weight can be 8061km (5009 miles), again depending on whether Pratt & Whitney JT9D-7 series engines are installed or other

Right: Roll-out of the first Boeing Model 747-300 for Swissair with an extended upper deck.

Above: The Australian airline Qantas has purchased two Boeing Model 747SP long-range transports.

types. Equally important is the Freighter's mechanical loading system, which allows a very small number of men to complete loading of the aircraft in half an hour.

The first Convertible flew in early 1973 but has proved less popular among operators in terms of the number ordered. It differs from the passenger 747 and the Freighter in having a standard fuselage with side windows plus the optional side cargo door but with an interior designed for all cargo operations in addition to all passenger or mixed loads. The Combi, on the other hand, has outsold both the Freighter and Convertible and offers a removable bulkhead to allow the interior layout to be organized for passengers only or for mixed loads of passengers/cargo, and has a large cargo door on the fuselage side as standard. The first new-production Combi was delivered for commercial service in early 1975.

Given the vast capacity of the 747 Freighter, it is perhaps surprising that more has not been made of its potential as a military hack. Clearly it is unsuited to the transportation of heavy military vehicles or outsized single items because of its high-from-the-ground nose loading door, but it is eminently suited to the bulk transportation of containerized goods or military spares such as aircraft engines. Such a military freighter, for example, could prove of immense use to the RAF for its Falklands air bridge once the planned new runways are completed, taking some of the strain from that service's Hercules transports and the flight refueling tankers needed to stretch their endurance. This aside, there is a military version of the 747 in USAF use, but this is flown as the E-4 advanced airborne command post to provide a communications link with US nuclear forces should conventional ground systems become inoperable due to interference or destruction.

The latest version of the basically standard 747 is the 747-300, which entered service in 1983. This is either a 747-100 or -200 series airliner with the upper deck area extended rearward to increase seating accommodation in interior for fewer passengers; and a high of 91. Alternatively, sleeper seats can be installed for fewer passengers. Also, by replacing the normal spiral stairs from the main deck to the upper deck with a straight stairway, seven extra seats can be installed on the main deck. The utilization of the upper deck area for passenger seats greatly increased the airliner's carrying capacity and therefore has made it potentially even more profitable for operators. But, as originally designed, this area was intended as a lounge for first-class passengers in a standard of luxury to rival that of the Boeing Stratocruiser radial-engined airliner of the 1940s and 1950s.

Two special versions of the Model 747 are the 747SP and 747SR. The latter is a Short-Range variant of the standard 747-100B, intended for use on shorter route services that have a high volume of traffic. Early examples had considerably lower maximum take-off weights than their standard counterparts but similar gross weights to 747-100Bs are currently offered. Most structural changes to the 747SR relate directly to the greater number of take-offs and landings expected of a shorter range airliner. The first SR was put into service in 1973.

The day prior to the first flight of a 747SR, 3 September 1973, Boeing announced that it was to develop a new variant to the existing 747 models. This was to become the Model 747SP, indicating Special Performance and giving airlines the opportunity of purchasing a 747 variant with longer than normal range for use on routes requiring fewer seats. The major structural change was to the fuselage, which was shortened by 14.35m (47ft 1in) to accommodate a maximum of 331 passengers. The reduced take-off weight of the 747SP, combined with a greater fuel capacity than for the 747-100B, allowed a demonstrated range of 10,841km (6736 miles) with a full passenger load at near maximum take-off weight.

The Model 747SP, which first appeared in mid-1975 and has since become a fairly common sight, cannot be said to be the most unusual 747. This title must surely go to the ex-American Airlines 747-123 modified for NASA as the piggy-back transporter for the Space Shuttle Orbiter.

Below: One of the USAF's Boeing E-4B airborne command post aircraft, deployed to provide a communications link with US forces should other systems become inoperable.

Left: Boeing's future success in the field of commercial airliners rests partly on its new Models 757 and 767.

Right: United Air Lines inaugurated commercial services with the Boeing 767-200 on 8 September 1982.

Above: Air Europe, the British inclusive tour operator, put the first of its two Boeing Model 757s into service on 22 April 1983.

Boeing's future success in the commercial airliner field rests to a large extent on its new Models 757 and 767, which have already attracted substantial orders from airlines. The wings of these new-generation airliners, like those of the most up-to-date types built by other companies such as Airbus Industrie in Europe, incorporate the latest technology and have less sweepback than previous aircraft of similar size. Coupled with very advanced turbofan engines, these airliners offer operators a very major reduction in the fuel burned in relation to seat-miles.

The first of the two Boeing aircraft to fly in prototype form was the widebodied Model 767, which took to the air initially on 26 September 1981. United Air Lines had been the first to order the 767, back in 1978, and therefore inaugurated commercial services with the type on 8 September 1982. Accommodation in the Model 767-200 initial version is for 211 passengers, although as many as 289 seats can be installed. All but two of the 174 airliners ordered by mid-1938 are variants of the standard 767-200, the two ordered by Ethiopian Airlines differing in being 767-200ERs, indicating the carriage of an increased fuel load for Extended Range.

Power for the 767s is provided either by two Pratt & Whitney JT9D-7R4D or General Electric CF6-80A turbofans, carried on pylons beneath the wings. Typical cruising speed and range are Mach 0.8 and 5522km (3431 miles) respectively, a medium range which can be increased greatly by the selection of higher weight or extended-range versions of the 767-200.

The company's much smaller Model 757 first flew on 19 February 1982 as a short/medium-range airliner intended to take over much of the business left by the Model 727, offering not only increased seating capacity over the older airliner but very substantial savings in operating costs. Its fuselage is modeled upon that of the 727, giving it a slim and long appearance, but in other respects it has a very different configuration. Its high-technology wings are sweptback at only 25 degrees, compared to 32 degrees for the 727, under which are carried two new gener-

ation turbofan engines. These can be either Rolls-Royce RB211-535C/E4s or Pratt & Whitney PW2037s. Because of the position of the engines, a T-tail is no longer required.

The basic version of the airliner is the 757-200, seating between 178 and 239 passengers. The first two customers, Eastern Air Lines and British Airways, inaugurated commercial services with the type respectively in January and February 1983, their aircraft using Rolls-Royce power plants. Orders for the 757 are split just about evenly between Rolls-Royce and Pratt & Whitney powered aircraft. Rolls-Royce models being balanced by a huge order for sixty 757s with PW2037 engines from Delta Air Lines and a small number from Transbrasil. Delta is expected to receive its first 757s in October 1984. Cruising speed of the 757 is similar to that of the 767, while range with 186 passengers on board is currently quoted at 4244km (2637 miles).

Boeing as a company began life as a military aircraft producer before American involvement in the First World War. Prior to the following world war Boeing was known equally for its civil and military aircraft, the latter including many famous fighters. The immediate run up years to the Second World War saw Boeing lean more to the development of large commercial and military aircraft, the outcome of which was the massive production of four-engined bombers during that war. The company's only major attempt of the war to get back into the naval single-seater field proved unsuccessful.

With turbojet engines available, Boeing got into postwar jet bomber production with its B-47 Stratojet, which entered service during the 1950s. Close on its tail was the eight-engined B-52 Stratofortress, first flown in 1952. Seven hundred and forty-four B-52s were built, the last coming off the production line more than twenty years ago. Yet, despite huge leaps forward in bomber technology over the ensuing years, the much reduced number of

Below: The USAF currently deploys operationally 241 Boeing B-52 Stratofortresses, the B-52H being the final version to be produced.

Right: The latest weapon earmarked for the Stratofortress is the Boeing Aerospace Company AGM-86B cruise missile.

Previous pages: A menacing night photograph of a Stratofortress.

of this comes with the projected modern B-1B bomber, which has a radar signature for an enemy to pick up one hundred times smaller than that of the B-52. With any prospect of having to cross enemy airspace that is perhaps guarded by ground warning radar, AWACS aircraft, thousands of antiaircraft missiles and hundreds of interceptors, the B-52's signature and slow speed must make this potentially extremely hazardous. However, as the stablemate of an entirely modern supersonic bomber with low observable technology, the B-52 could still have an important role to play for some years to come.

Currently operational with the USAF

heavy loads of conventional weapons. Defense against attack from the rear is accomplished by the use of four 0.50in machine-guns in a tail turret on the B-52G and a single 20mm cannon on the B-52H. The remaining 40 B-52s not marked for ALCM have been used to supersede the B-52D (withdrawn from operational service) in a non-nuclear maritime support capacity, soon to carry Harpoon anti-shipping missiles. This new role for the Stratofortress has not been practiced by the US services since the days of the B-17 Flying Fortress but has been a standard duty of Soviet heavy bombers for a very long time.

B-52s that remain in service represent the USAF's and NATO's only long-range heavy strategic bomber force. It is probably the bomber's fairly modern appearance that helps give credence to the opinion expressed in some circles that the B-52 can be relied on for ever, yet this illusion can be dispelled simply by stating known facts. For example, the development and deployment of more and more sophisticated defense systems have very much diminished the possibility of older-style aircraft like the B-52 reaching their assigned targets, even though regularly updated with new avionics and weapons. Proof

are 241 B-52G and Hs, all of which have been the subject of modernization programs over the years. The majority are being, or have been, further updated to have the Offensive Avionics System (OAS) fitted which improves navigation and weapon delivery for low-altitude penetration missions. Another program currently underway involves modification of 201 G/Hs to carry the new AGM-86 air-launched cruise missile, each aircraft supporting twelve under its wings, supplemented by eight SRAM missiles carried on a rotary launcher inside the bomb-bay and free-fall bombs. As an alternative, B-52s can carry

The B-52G and H differ mainly in the engines fitted, the former having eight Pratt & Whitney J57-P-43WB turbojets carried in pairs on long forward-swept pylons and the latter having eight slightly more powerful Pratt & Whitney TF33-P-3 turbofans. Maximum speed of the Stratofortress is 957km/h (595mph) and ranges without flight refueling are about 12,070km (7500 miles) and 16,090km (10,000 miles) respectively.

Traditionally Boeing has had two great US rivals in the airliner manufacturing business, namely Lockheed and Douglas. Back in 1933, when Boeing produced the prototype of what is generally recognized as having been the first modern airliner, the Model 247, Douglas developed the rival DC-1 and -2 and Lockheed produced its L.10 Electra, all with seating for between ten and fourteen passengers. It is arguable which of these companies produced the ultimate piston-engined airliner postwar, the Boeing Stratocruiser, Douglas DC-6 and -7, and the Lockheed Constellation/Super Constellation/Starliner series all setting very high standards of safety and luxury. After Lockheed developed and manufactured its L-188 Electra with turbo-prop engines, as detailed in the opening chapter, the company only re-entered the airliner market again with the L-1011 TriStar, the first example of which flew on 16 November 1970.

The TriStar was the world's third type of wide-bodied jetliner to fly. Its original design was partly based on the known requirements of American Airlines, although in the event this operator subsequently chose to purchase Lockheed's rival 'triple' in the form of the DC-10. For its new airliner, Lockheed selected (in March 1968) the emerging Rolls-Royce RB.211 turbofan, two of which were to be carried under the wings and one in the rear fuselage. However, the enormous cost of development of this advanced engine actually brought about the collapse of Rolls-Royce, which was re-formed in 1971 using British government backing.

The first TriStar flew initially on 16 November 1970 and in April 1972 Eastern Air Lines inaugurated passenger services with the type. However, the TriStar for early commercial use was fitted with RB.211-22C engines, the standard RB.211-22B not being certificated until the following year,

at which time the 'Cs' were uprated to 'B' standard.

As a follow on to the L-1011-1 basic version accommodating up to 400 passengers, Lockheed manufactured the L-1011-100 and -200 extended range versions, the latter with more powerful RB.211-524 series engines. Similar engines were fitted to the final production version, the L-1011-500. By far the heaviest version, with a greatly in-creased fuel capacity, it was offered with accommodation for up to 330 passengers in a shortened fuselage. The first operator of the -500 was British Airways, which introduced it onto its routes in May 1979. Maximum cruising speed at 9150m (30,000ft) and full load range of the L-1011-1 and -500 are respectively 964km/h (599mph) and 973km/h (605mph), and 4965km (3086 miles) and 9905km (6154 miles).

Below: Cathay Pacific Airways, based in Hong Kong, is one of the many operators of the Lockheed L-1011 TriStar.

Right: The shorter fuselage but longer range L-1011-500 TriStar was ordered by ten airlines, including BWIA International.

Due to the depressed state of the world airliner market during the recession and other factors, Lockheed decided to end production of the TriStar in 1984 after completion of aircraft on order. By the beginning of 1983 a total of 237 had been delivered to customers around the world. Ex-civil TriStars are ports, a service which is eventually expected to deploy six as flight refueling eventually deploy six as flight refueling tankers. Deletion of the TriStar from Lockheed's production lines in 1984 will mean that the company will not be offering a commercial passenger airliner among its range of products, although it will still have the L-100 series commercial Hercules to keep alive its civil aircraft interests.

Lockheed's military jets are varied indeed and include a still secret single-seat fighter and reconnaissance aircraft incorporating the new low observable technology, constructed at the company's famous Skunk Works at Burbank and reportedly designated XF-19. The Skunk Works has been responsible for the design and development of several highly significant aircraft over several decades, including Lockheed's well-known F-104 Starfighter. It was the company's proposal for a very high altitude strategic reconnaissance version of the Starfighter to overfly enemy territory that led to the original U-2, a relatively small number of which were delivered for operational service during the 1950s.

In 1968 a new and more powerful version of the U-2 was put into produc-

tion as the U-2R, still retaining the aircraft's typical straight and very wide span wings to allow gliding flight to preserve fuel. It is known that two further U-2Rs have recently been built. Also in production in the early 1980s has been the TR-1A, a single-seat tactical reconnaissance variant of the U-2 of which the USAF requires 33 plus two two-seat trainers (TR-1B). Each TR-1A has a single Pratt & Whitney J57-P-13B turbojet engine and the necessary electronic sensors to allow all-weather surveillance by day or night. More than half the TR-1s are expected to be based in Europe, each carrying advanced ECM and with side-looking airborne radar to provide the required information without the necessity of an overflight. Cruising speed of the TR-1A is

Below: The final production version of the Lockheed Starfighter was the F-104S, a multi-mission aircraft license-built in Italy by Aeritalia.

690km/h (430mph), operating ceiling is 27,435m (90,000ft), and it has a maximum endurance of 12 hours.

On the other end of the speed scale for reconnaissance duties is another Skunk Works aircraft in the form of the SR-71A, a Mach 3+ two-seat strategic reconnaissance aircraft which can claim to be the fastest military aircraft in operational use today. Powered by two Pratt & Whitney J58 turbojet engines, this unarmed aircraft can photograph 259,000sq km (100,000sq miles) of territory in one hour or undertake more specialized surveillance missions. Entering USAF service from 1966, only a small number was built. An interceptor of similar overall configuration was also flown in prototype form but this did not reach pro-

Left: A new and
refined tactical
reconnaissance version
of the U-2 is the
Lockheed TR-1A,
capable of operating at
an altitude of about
27,435m (90,000ft).

Below: Still the fastest
aircraft in service
today is the Lockheed
SR-71A, which can
photograph 259,000 sq
km (100,000 sq miles)
of territory in an hour.

duction status. A remotely piloted vehicle (RPV) of similar appearance to the manned aircraft but smaller, yet capable of Mach 3+ reconnaissance missions when launched from Boeing B-52 bombers, achieved operational use for some years under the designation GTD-21.

Lockheed's strong links with naval aircraft have resulted in the production of several maritime patrol and anti-submarine aircraft with piston or turboprop engines as their main power plants, including the Orion/Aurora. Between 1974 and 1978 Lockheed also delivered to the US Navy 187 examples of its S-3A Viking, a four-seat and twin General Electric TF34 turbofan-engined anti-submarine aircraft suited to operation from aircraft carriers. Its maximum speed and combat range are 833km/h (518mph) and over 3700km (2300 miles) respectively, and each Viking is packed with modern avionics and carries torpedoes, mines, depth charges, rockets and other weapons in its fuselage bays and underwing to attack submerged or surface vessels once detected.

Two new versions of the Viking have been projected: the KS-3 on-board flight refueling tanker and the US-3A carrier on-board delivery (COD) shore-to-ship transport. And it is in the field of

military transports that Lockheed can probably claim greatest success, its products having included the turbo-prop-powered C-130 Hercules that has been in worldwide service since the late 1950s. Another is the C-141 Star-Lifter, a capacious transport that has recently undergone a 'stretch' to increase the carrying ability of all 270 flown by Military Airlift Command, as well as providing each with inflight refueling capability. These are now known under the USAF designation

Above: One of the US Navy's Lockheed S-3A Viking anti-submarine aircraft comes in to land on a carrier deck.

Below: One of Military Airlift Command's Lockheed C-141B StarLifter transports in the new camouflage scheme.

Right: StarLifters operating as paratroop transports.

C-141B. Four Pratt & Whitney TF33-P-7 turbofan engines produce the power to lift a payload of 41,220kg (90,880lb), and allow a maximum cruising speed of 910km/h (566mph) and range with a full load of 4725km (2935 miles).

Undoubtedly the company's major triumph in the field of large military transport aircraft has been the design and manufacture for operational service of the gargantuan C-5 Galaxy, still the world's largest production aircraft and possibly only rivaled by the new Soviet Antonov An-400 that was undergoing flight tests in 1983.

Design of the Galaxy started in the early 1960s when manufacturers were requested to propose aircraft capable of transporting a payload of 56,700kg (125,000lb) over a range of 12,875km (8000 miles), yet be suited to existing runways. Lockheed was subsequently selected winner among the competing proposals and the first C-5A Galaxy flew initially on 30 June 1968. Today

the USAF has 77 in operational use, each powered by four large General Electric TF39-GE-C turbofan engines carried under the massive 67.88m (222ft 8½in)-span wings. The length of the aircraft is equally impressive, at 75.54m (247ft 10in), and the maximum payload of 120,065kg (264,700lb) can be made up of 345 troops or typically either two main battle tanks, sixteen small trucks, helicopters, ten Pershing tactical missiles with wheeled launch and support vehicles, or a large number of other cargoes, loaded through the aircraft's lift-up nose. Cruising speed can be 908km/h (564mph) and range up to 11,025km (6850 miles).

A further 50 Galaxies are expected to be constructed for the USAF under the revised designation C-5B, the first entering service in 1985. These will incorporate the new advanced and strengthened wings currently being retrofitted to C-5As. The purchase of these incredibly expensive aircraft,

together with the recent 'stretching' of the StarLifter, gives some indication of the US forces' continuing commitment to massive transport capability, intended to reinforce peacetime troop levels and armor on a global basis.

The present day McDonnell Douglas Corporation evolved from a 1967 merger of the McDonnell Company and the Douglas Aircraft Company. The latter is, therefore, a division of the McDonnell Douglas Corporation and is responsible for its commercial airliners and military transports. In the military field its main current product is the KC-10A Extender, a flight refueling tanker based on the DC-10 airliner, which is also capable of transporting 76,825kg (169,370lb) of cargo in a conventional transport role. The KC-10A entered USAF service in 1981 and 20

Below: The Lockheed C-5A Galaxy is currently the world's largest operational aircraft, but might soon be rivalled by the new Soviet An-400.

Above: A McDonnell Douglas KC-10A Extender refueling an A-4M Skyhawk from the Naval Air Test Center.

Left: The first McDonnell Douglas DC-8 Super 71 airliners were delivered in the spring of 1982.

Above: McDonnell Douglas MD-80s have been in commercial service since October 1980.

Inset: KLM is a major European operator of the McDonnell Douglas DC-10.

have been built. The company has also proposed its C-17 as a future long-range military transport, combining a capacious cargo interior to accommodate the largest items of military equipment with STOL performance. However, there seems little chance of the C-17 going into production in this decade.

The Douglas Aircraft Company division of McDonnell Douglas is, of course, best known for its civil airliners. The company entered the jet age with its DC-8, which first appeared in 1958 as a rival to the Boeing Model 707. Production of the DC-8 ended more than a decade ago but since then modification work has resulted in new versions for freighting and passenger carrying. The most important of these are the DC-8 Super 71, 72 and 73, in fact production DC-8 Super 61, 62 and 63 airliners re-engined with four CFM International CFM56-2-1C turbofan engines offering performance improvements and a very substantial reduction in noise levels. Accommodation remains up to 259 passengers for the Super 73 but cruising speed at 10,670m (35,000ft) altitude is 855km/h (531mph) and range with a full load is 8950km (5560 miles).

Unlike Boeing, which developed a fairly large capacity trijet to satisfy the short/medium-range airliner market, Douglas went for a smaller capacity twin-turbofan design. This became the DC-9. Delta Air Lines inaugurated DC-9 services in November 1965, using the initial 90-seat version. Production of the initial Series 10 ended some years ago, as did the similar Series 20 optimized for use in hot climates or from high-altitude airports. Current standard models are the larger Series 30 accommodating up to 119 passengers, Series 40 with seats for 132 passengers in a still longer fuselage, and the Series 50. The latter is the longest version, with an overall length of 40.72m (133ft 7¼in), a massive increase when compared to the 31.82m (104ft 4¾in) length of the Series 10. Accommodation is raised to a maximum of 139 passengers in a restyled interior. The first Series 50 was put into service in 1975. Maximum cruising speed of the Series 50 is 898km/h (558mph) and range while carrying 97 passengers is typically 3325km (2067 miles). Mixed passenger/cargo and convertible variants of the DC-9 models are also available.

Apart from these standard versions of the DC-9, the former Super 30 and Super 80 are now known as the MD-90 and MD-80 respectively under the company's new designation system. The MD-90 is intended for operation over shorter range routes requiring a lower density of seating. It is therefore projected with an overall length fixed between those of the DC-9 Series 30 and 40, to accommodate up to 125 passengers. However, this is not expected to be in commercial use until the second half of this decade.

The MD-90 will be powered by two Pratt & Whitney JT8D-218 turbofan engines, which offer reduced noise levels and better fuel economy over the earlier JT8Ds of standard DC-9 versions. JT8D-200 series engines are also standard on the MD-80, the longest DC-9 type, intended to carry up to 172 passengers over short to medium ranges. Two versions of the MD-80 are already in service, namely the basic MD-81 and the more powerful MD-82, while the longer-range MD-83 will be inaugurated into commercial operation in 1985. The MD-81, which was first to be seen in Swissair colors in 1980, has a maximum speed of 926km/h (575mph) and a range with maximum fuel load of 4925km (3060 miles).

Not to be forgotten in the standard DC-9 series are the military derivatives, flown as the USAF's C-9A Nightingale aeromedical transport for up to 40 stretchers or ambulatory patients and the VC-9C VIP transport, and the US Navy's C-9B Skytrain II transport. Two Skytrain IIs also serve with the Kuwait Air Force as VIP transports.

McDonnell Douglas' largest ever production airliner is the DC-10, already mentioned in its KC-10A Extender military version. Indeed, such has been the state of the airliner market during the recession that production of the Extender has kept the production line working and has allowed the company the opportunity of keeping the DC-10 available for purchase.

The DC-10 was the second type of US wide-bodied jetliner and the first trijet wide-body, beating the Lockheed Tri-Star into the air by less than three months. Its success has, to a large extent, been based on the ability of versions to operate economically over very short, medium and long routes while carrying between 255 and 380 passengers.

The DC-10 Series 10 was the first version offered, which was inaugurated into service by American Airlines in 1971. The later Series 15, 30 and 30ER have also each been powered by a version of the General Electric CF6 turbofan, although these subsequent models of the airliner have been progressively more powerful, with higher gross weights and offering longer ranges. Only the Series 40 uses non General Electric engines, changing to three Pratt & Whitney JT9D turbofans. This model was evolved for operation over intercontinental routes and is therefore the longest-range version of all, capable of up to 7500km (4663 miles) while carrying a full passenger load. The maximum cruising speed of the Series 40 is also high, at up to 922km/h (573mph), although this is slightly lower than the maximum cruising speed for the Series 10. Convertible passenger/cargo variants of the Series 10 and 30 are also offered. A future airliner based on the DC-10 is company designated MD-100. Two versions are envisaged for service from 1987/88, each with the latest technology turbofan engines, configurational, constructional and other changes to include drag-reducing winglets. The Series 10 variant is to be shorter than existing DC-10s and will carry 270 passengers in a mixed class layout, while the Series 20 will be the longest of any DC-10/MD-100 type with seating for 333 persons. Each MD-100 variant will have long range at full passenger load.

has received 138. These were either assembled or built in Japan by Mitsubishi. Indeed, the very last Phantom II constructed anywhere was a JASDF aircraft delivered on 20 May 1981.

At the time of writing only one US aircraft carrier squadron still flys Phantom IIs the type having been largely superseded by the modern Grumman F-14 Tomcat. Nevertheless, the Phantom still plays an important role with the USAF and many foreign air forces and has fairly recently been supplied to Egypt as part of that nations re-equipment with western aircraft. Although in the long term the RAF (now the only British service to fly the Phantom following the scrapping of HMS *Ark Royal*) will have its F-4s replaced by examples of the air defense variant of the European Panavia Tor-

Left: The McDonnell Aircraft Division of McDonnell Douglas delivered 5057 Phantom IIs before production ended in late 1979, the illustrated aircraft being the 5000th off the St Louis production line.

Right: The impressive weapon carrying capability of the McDonnell Douglas F-15 Eagle in an air-to-air role is well illustrated by this aircraft, which has four AIM-7F Sparrow and four smaller AIM-9L Sidewinder missiles.

Below: The sun sets on an F-15C Eagle of the 36th Tactical Fighter Wing, USAFE, stationed in West Germany.

The McDonnell Aircraft division of McDonnell Douglas Corporation is the current combat plane-producing side of the company, its recently out of production aircraft including the internationally flown F-4 Phantom II. The prototype Phantom II, conceived as a two-seat long-range fighter for the US Navy, flew for the first time on 27 May 1958. The US Navy began deployment of its F-4B version in 1961, and this was followed by the USAF's F-4C fighter-bomber derivative. The F-4B/F-4C were only the initial versions of the Phantom II. By the close of the production line in the USA in 1979, the US Navy had received more than 1260 (including those for the US Marine Corps), the USAF had acquired nearly 2600 over the years and a further 1196 had been exported to NATO and other countries, recipients including Great Britain and West Germany. Another customer was the Japan Air Self-Defense Force, which nado, it remains at present the most important British fighter, based on the Falkland Islands as well as in Europe. Other NATO countries operating F-4s include West Germany, Greece, Spain and Turkey. Maximum speed of the F-4 on the power of its two General Electric J79 turbojet engines is over Mach 2 and its combat radius for a strike mission is 1145km (712 miles). The weapon load is typically air-to-air missiles or up to 7250kg (16,000lb) of ground

Below: The Enhanced Eagle demonstrator loaded with ground attack weapons and Sidewinder missiles for self defense.

Above: This A-4M was the very last Skyhawk produced, specially painted to carry the colors of operating nations.

attack weapons carried on four under-fuselage stations and a further four under the wings. The Phantom II is particularly easy to recognize due to the dihedral on the outer wing panels and the anhedral tailplane.

Work on a replacement for the USAF's Phantom IIs began in the 1960s, resulting in the development and selection for service of the McDonnell Douglas F-15 Eagle. Unlike the US Navy/USMC's chosen F-4 replacement, the Eagle has fixed wings and is a single seater (except for the tandem two-seat training variants). The first development F-15 flew on 27 July 1972, followed nearly a year later by the first two seater. Deliveries to the USAF began in late 1974 and to date nearly 800 have gone into service of an expected total of 1488. Some of these have been assigned to the US Rapid Deployment Force.

Eagles have also been exported to Israel (40) and the JASDF is receiving 100, the majority of the latter being constructed in Japan by Mitsubishi. Israeli F-15s took part in the attack on Iraq's nuclear reactor in mid-1981, then under construction at Osirak. Six pro-vided fighter cover for an attack force of F-16s.

Air superiority is the main role for the Eagle, although it can be used to deliver up to 7257kg (16,000lb) of attack weapons in a change of mission. But, for specialized attack, McDonnell Douglas has developed an F-15 derivative known as the Enhanced Eagle, whose main mission is interdiction but has a secondary air superiority capability. To date the Enhanced Eagle remains a prototype but it could be selected by the USAF for service in the future. In the meantime production of

Below: A McDonnell Douglas F/A-18 Hornet from a Naval Test and Evaluation Squadron comes in to land on a carrier deck with its arrester hook lowered.

the standard Eagle goes on, the single-seat F-15A and two-seat F-15B having been superseded on production lines by the F-15C and D respectively in 1979. These latest versions retain the same overall configuration of the F-15A/B and the two Pratt & Whitney F100-PW-100 turbofan engines, but, in addition to increased internal fuel capacity, they can have FAST Packs attached to the sides of the fuselage air intakes. These Packs are specially shaped streamline auxiliary fuel tanks which can also house a wide variety of electronic equipment for reconnaissance, ECM and other missions. They do not detract from the Eagle's Mach 2.5+ performance capability and increase the aircraft's maximum range, for long non-combat ferry flights from 4631km (2878 miles) to 5560km (3450 miles). Armament can be a 20mm multi-barrel cannon plus eight air-to-air missiles.

McDonnell has had, throughout its jet combat aircraft production career, a close association with naval aircraft in addition to land-based types. It was responsible for the US Navy's first jet fighters for carrier operations, in the form of the FH-1 Phantom (first flown in 1945), the F2H Banshee (1947) and the F3H Demon (1951). In 1979 McDonnell Douglas produced the 2960th and last A-4 Skyhawk, a single seat attack bomber originally conceived in the 1950s to meet a US Navy requirement for a low-cost and lightweight aircraft powered by a single turbojet engine. Most production Skyhawks use a Pratt & Whitney J52 engine and, in addition to two 20mm cannon, can carry various weapon loads up to a 4535kg (10,000lb) maximum weight. Many Skyhawks were exported for carrier and land-based operation and some, like those flown by the Royal Australian Navy, can launch Sidewinder air-to-air missiles.

The company's latest combat aircraft for the US Navy is the F/A-18 Hornet, like the Skyhawk intended primarily as a carrier aircraft but for strike and fighter roles. It was based strongly on Northrop's YF-17, a lightweight fighter prototype of the early 1970s that failed to be selected by the USAF against the competing YF-16 from General Dynamics. First flown on 18 November 1978, the Hornet is in production for the US Navy and US Marine Corps as a Phantom II, Skyhawk and Corsair II replacement and is built in single-seat F/A-18A and two-seat TF/A-18A training forms. The Canadian Armed Forces are also receiving Hornets as CF-18s to supersede Canadair-built versions of the Lockheed F-104 Starfighter and Northrop F-5 and the McDonnell CF-101F Voodoo, while Royal Australian Air Force

F/A-18As are to take over fighter duties from the French Dassault-Breguet Mirage III-0. The Spanish Air Force is yet another user. Total USN/USMC procurement of the Hornet could well exceed 1300 by the 1990s.

The Northrop YF-17 had a 'clean' gross weight of 10,430kg (23,000lb) and a maximum speed in excess of Mach 2. The Hornet, powered by two General Electric F404-GE-400 turbofans, weighs in at 15,740kg (34,700lb) when armed as a fighter or 22,316kg (49,200lb) when carrying up to 7710kg (17,000lb) of weapons for a strike mission. Maximum speed also reflects the aircraft's heavier weight, despite greater engine power than provided for the YF-17, at Mach 1.8+. In attack configuration the Hornet's combat radius is 1065km (662 miles).

McDonnell Douglas is also heavily committed to two aircraft of British origin, namely the Harrier and Hawk. The latter tandem two-seat jet trainer was developed for the RAF by Hawker Siddeley/British Aerospace and has enjoyed export success. To meet a US Navy requirement for a new jet trainer, and reflecting the US Congress' predilection for usually funding only those aircraft involving US manufacturing companies, McDonnell Douglas is heading the Hawk VTXTS program. This will eventually produce the initial T-45B, a land-based Americanized Hawk trainer of which 54 will be procured, to be followed by perhaps more than 250 T-45As capable of operating from aircraft carriers. T-45As will, therefore, incorporate several modifications new to the Hawk, including a new undercarriage and an arrester hook, but a present contentious point is the Congress' insistence that the British Martin-Baker ejection seats have to be replaced with US seats.

McDonnell Douglas' involvement with the Harrier is in the joint program with British Aerospace to develop and produce the Harrier II. This follow-on version to the present Harrier, as used mainly by the US Marine Corps and RAF, has been evolved to double the weapon carrying capability/range of the Harrier without the necessity of designing a new airframe or producing a costly new engine. As it has been more closely based on USMC requirements than the type of follow-on aircraft originally conceived for the RAF, the Harrier II is more of a 'bomb truck' than a higher performance, better man-

Below: A swarm of Hornets from test squadrons over Nevada in 1983.

Right: This McDonnell Douglas/BAe AV-8B Harrier II lifts into the air with sixteen 570lb bombs.

euvering and longer range version of the existing Harrier considered best for the new RAF version that was being developed a few years ago in Britain under the name Big Wing Harrier. It is still probably true that, despite some features of the Big Wing Harrier being incorporated into Harrier II (such as the leading-edge root extensions to the wings to improve the instantaneous rate of turn), USMC and RAF requirements are still not entirely the same and Britain accepts the Americanized Harrier II mainly because of the USMC's large orders which will reduce unit costs. If this requires substantiating, the Falklands war proved the necessity for attack aircraft to possess

high performance and good maneuverability to survive in a modern battle environment. Nevertheless, range has been increased for the Harrier II and certainly the greater weapon carrying capability, which stands at 4173kg (9200lb), is a great improvement.

Other features of the Harrier II include the substantial use of carbon-fiber composite materials in the construction of parts of the airframe, the use of supercritical wings and high-lift devices, and a new cockpit to give improved visibility to the pilot. Production AV-8B Harrier IIs have already been delivered to the USMC, although the first units will not become operational until 1985, and it is expected that

more than 250 will be purchased initially. RAF Harrier GR.Mk 5s, differing from USMC aircraft in having two 30mm Aden cannon and not the US 25mm General Electric GAU-12/U multi-barrel cannon, will be acquired from 1986. The only other Harrier operating nation, Spain, will also receive 12 AV-8Bs to expand its existing V/STOL force of AV-8A Matadors that are flown from the aircraft carrier *Dédalo*. The Harrier IIs will undoubtedly be flown from the new Spanish Navy carrier *Principe de Asturias*. Maximum speed of the Harrier II on the power of its single Rolls-Royce Pegasus 11 Mk 103 vectored thrust turbofan engine is 1075km/h (668mph) at sea level.

CHAPTER THREE
BUSINESS, BOMBERS, BARRIER-BREAKERS
AMERICAN ENTERPRISE

This heading is close to a summary of chapter three, which details the remaining jet aircraft of US manufacture. The companies included differ fundamentally from those in the second chapter by currently producing only civil *or* military jet aircraft, while making some allowance for basically civil types that have found a small measure of success in military circles.

Back in 1973, Bede Aircraft Incorporated of Kansas put onto the market plans, component parts and materials for the construction by amateur builders of a diminutive single-seat jet under the designation BD-5J. With a wing span of only 5.18m (17ft) and an overall length of just 3.78m (12ft 4¾in), this 'homebuilt' proved capable of 444km/h (276mph) on the power from a single 92kg (202lb) thrust Microturbo TRS 18 turbojet engine. A factory-built version later appeared as the BD-5JP. Although these are no longer available for purchase, examples can be seen in the hands of enthusiasts and one was used in thrilling moments of the James Bond film *Octopussy*.

More conventional civil jets are the aircraft of the Citation series, the first commercial-market jet products of the Cessna Aircraft Company. The original

Seven- to nine-seat Cessna Citation I executive transport.

Inset: Bede BD-5J, the world's smallest jet aircraft.

Below: The high-speed Gates Learjet 25D, capable of 880km/h (547mph), flying above a Learjet 35A.

Citation first took to the air as a prototype twin-turbofan executive/business transport in 1969. The Citation I available today accommodates seven to nine persons, including the pilot, and offers the luxury interior items expected of this class of aircraft, including a refreshment unit, table, luxury seats, special lighting arrangements, toilet, curtains and so on. The two rear fuselage-mounted Pratt & Whitney Aircraft of Canada JT15D-1B turbofan engines allow a cruising speed of 662km/h (411mph) and a typical range of 2461km (1529 miles).

The slightly larger and more powerful Citation II first appeared at the beginning of 1977. It can cruise at higher speed and accommodates a crew of two and up to ten passengers. Like the Citation I, a single-pilot model is also available.

The latest Cessna executive jet is the longer-range Citation III, which is most easily identifiable by its T-tail structure. Accommodating six to nine passengers, the two Garrett TFE731-3B-100S turbofan engines give the Citation III a maximum cruising speed of 874km/h (543mph), taking it into the league of the high-speed executive jets that are typified by the Learjets from the Gates Learjet Corporation.

The Gates Learjet Corporation was founded in 1970 from the previous Lear Jet Corporation, the latter which had been marketing the Learjet 23 and 24 high-speed executive jets. Production of the six-passenger Learjet 24F, the final version of the 24 series, ended in 1980. Today the company offers its Learjet 25D, an eight-passenger (plus two crew) jet powered by two rear fuselage-mounted General Electric CJ610-8A turbojets and capable of 880km/h (547mph), the better equipped and longer range Learjet 25G, and the twin Garrett TFE731-3A-2B turbofan Learjet 55. Only recently has the company ended production of the Learjet 35A and 36A, which are a little larger than the Learjet 25 and use turbofan power.

The Learjet 55 first appeared in prototype form in 1979 and deliveries started in 1981. Unlike earlier Learjets, the 55 offers seating for up to eight passengers in a wide-body type forward fuselage with stand-up height. Another new feature to the Learjet series is the use of supercritical winglets on the

Left: The B-1B will have an airframe hardened to help it survive in a nuclear blast environment and will incorporate 'low observable' technology.

Below left: Wings swept for high speed flight, the B-1B is expected to be fully capable of penetrating sophisticated enemy defenses well into the next decade.

or other chosen loads that can comprise 38 short range attack missiles (SRAMs) or $128 \times 500lb$ conventional high-explosive bombs. The added conventional capability for the B-1B has greatly increased the range of conflict scenarios in which the bomber could play a useful role, especially in view of the importance attached to its low altitude penetration role at high subsonic speed.

The most obvious external feature of the B-1B is its huge variable geometry wings which, when spread, bestow on the bomber the ability to take off quickly from shorter length airfields and fly at low speeds. For high subsonic or supersonic (up to Mach 1.25) speeds, the wings are swept at 67° 30'. The former air conditioned and pressurized flight compartment of the B-1, that served also as an emergency escape capsule for the four-man crew, has been one casualty of the initial aim to reduce unit costs, and on the B-1B the crew have individual ejection seats. However, the B-1B airframe is hardened to help it survive in a nuclear blast environment. Power is provided by four General Electric F101-GE-102 turbofan engines and the aircraft's unrefueled range is about 12,000km (7450 miles).

Returning briefly to business/executive jets manufactured in the North American continent, Canadair in Quebec has been achieving considerable success with its Challenger business and commuter/cargo twin-jet. Developed from a design by William Lear of Learjet fame, the Challenger first flew as a prototype in November 1978. Today two versions are in production for customers, both of which can accommodate up to 19 passengers. The CL-600 Challenger basic variant is powered by two rear fuselage-mounted Avco Lycoming ALF502L turbofan engines, which bestow a maximum cruising speed of 833km/h (518mph). A range of 5925km (3682 miles) is possible when the aircraft is carrying its maximum fuel load, allowing for reserve fuel. The CL-601 has more powerful General Electric CF34-1A turbofans and features winglets on the advanced design wings.

Back in 1966 the twin-turbofan Grumman Gulfstream II appeared as a large business jet for up to 19 passengers. This entered production and more than 250 were completed before 1979, when

tips of the slightly sweptback wings. Four versions are marketed, the ER (extended range), LR (long range) and XLR (extra long range), in addition to the standard Learjet 55. The XLR's greatly increased fuel tankage allows a range of 4761km (2958 miles) with the maximum four passengers. Maximum speed of the Learjet 55 is 884km/h (549mph).

Between December 1979 and 1981 Rockwell Internation's Sabreliner Division manufactured what was to become the final version of the Sabreliner series of twin-jet business aircraft, the Sabreliner 65. Fitted with supercritical wings, powered by two Garrett TFE731-3-1D turbofan engines mounted on the rear of the fuselage and accommodating eight passengers, it is now just one of the Sabreliner models supported by the Sabreliner Corporation, a company formed in 1983 following Rockwell International's sale of this Division.

The Rockwell International Corporation's major aircraft program at the present time is the development and production of the B-1B, the long-range strategic bomber that is intended for USAF service from 1986. The B-1B has been based on the company's earlier B-1, of which 240 full-production examples (each capable of speeds in excess of Mach 2.2) would now be in operational use had President Carter not canceled the program in 1977.

The B-1B, of which 100 have been authorized by President Reagan for delivery up to 1988, is slower than the B-1 and heavier. However, it incorporates the added advantages of the latest avionics, a strengthened structure to take account of a substantial increase in the gross weight, a greater weapon load capability, and incorporates low observable technology to ensure that the radar signature it gives off to an enemy is one-hundredth that of the B-52 Stratofortress.

Originally conceived as a lower cost carrier-plane for air launched cruise missiles, further consideration of the B-1B's potential led to the decision to allow it to perform more conventional strategic roles in addition to that of ALCM carrier. Now the B-1B's impressive load will include 22 ALCMs among the weapons carried in the internal bays and under the fuselage, the assembly line was closed. By this time the Grumman American Aviation Corporation, a subsidiary of the Grumman Corporation, had been taken over by American Jet Industries and the current resulting company is named the Gulfstream Aerospace Corporation. Work had, by the time of the take-over, begun on the superseding and longer-range Gulfstream III, featuring a lengthened fuselage and new wings with winglets. Power is provided by two Rolls-Royce Spey Mk 511-8 turbofan engines, which allow a speed and typical range with eight passengers of 927km/h (576mph) and 6759km (4200 miles) respectively. Military examples of the Gulfstream III cover a small number that have been acquired by the

USAF as Special Air Missions Task aircraft to replace Lockheed JetStars, and three are used by the Royal Danish Air Force for fishery patrol and other maritime duties.

Gulfstream Aerospace is currently working on an update of the Gulfstream III, known as the Gulfstream IV, to be powered by Rolls-Royce RB.183 Tay turbofan engines. A totally new executive jet from the company is the Commander Fanjet 1500, which flew for the first time in January 1983. A six-to eight-seat aircraft, it features unusual down-canted winglets and a large air intake above the fuselage for the single Pratt & Whitney Aircraft of Canada JT15D turbofan engine. Delivery of production Fanjet 1500s is some way ahead.

Mitsubishi is a name more readily associated with Japan and indeed MAI (Mitsubishi Aircraft International) is a subsidiary of Mitsubishi Heavy Industries of Tokyo. However, during the

1970s MAI became fully based in the USA. One of its products is the Diamond I, a seven-passenger executive jet capable of 797km/h (495mph) on the power of two Pratt & Whitney Aircraft of Canada JT15D-4 turbofan engines. The Diamond I, only operated since 1982, has already been superseded by the marginally more powerful Diamond IA.

In the field of combat aircraft, no other is more unusual in configuration than the Fairchild Republic A-10A Thunderbolt II. This single seater, a 704km/h (438mph) tank-buster and bomb/missile-carrying close support aircraft, has broken new ground with the USAF and many believe it responsible in part for the development in the Soviet Union of a similar aircraft that is known to NATO as *Frogfoot*.

As a prototype, the A-10A first flew on 10 May 1972 and then went on to win production orders for the USAF against Northrop's quite different A-9A. Operational deployment began in 1977, when

Below: One of the three Gulfstream Aerospace Gulfstream IIIs operated by the Royal Danish Air Force for fishery patrol and other maritime duties.

Canadair's remarkably successful
CL-600 Challenger business and
commuter/cargo transport, developed
from a design by William Lear.

Above: One of the most important weapons carried by the A-10A is the Maverick, a precision target missile that can be launched against heavily armored vehicles and fortified positions.

Left: Good camouflage is essential to the survivability of the A-10A in the battle area.

Below right: Full-scale mock-up of the Fairchild Republic T-46A trainer.

Below: Lined-up for a training mission in Egypt are Fairchild Republic A-10A Thunderbolt IIs of the 353rd Tactical Fighter Squadron, USAF.

the 356th Tactical Fighter Squadron, 354th Tactical Fighter Wing, became combat ready. In 1979 the first A-10As arrived in England, where more than 100 are stationed today for emergency basing in West Germany. Production of the A-10A has ended, a total of more than 700 having been delivered to the USAF.

Powered by two General Electric TF34-GE-100 turbofan engines, that are mounted in pods on the rear fuselage to exhaust through the twin fin and rudder tail unit, the A-10A's heart is a huge and devastating General Electric GAU-8/A Avenger 30mm seven-barrel cannon. Installed in the forward fuselage and protruding from the nose, the Avenger cannon is capable of defeating medium battle tanks and other armor. Added to this weapon can be up to 7257kg (16,000lb) of bombs, missiles or other stores carried on the under fuselage and underwing stations. A common weapon is the Maverick, a precision target missile that can be used against heavily armored vehicles and fortified positions. In action, the A-10A can operate at very low level to surprise enemy positions while in support of friendly ground forces. It can use electronic countermeasures to locate enemy radar positions and to warn the pilot that hostile ground forces have locked onto the aircraft in readiness to launch an antiaircraft missile. Camouflage is used to reduce its visibility to other aircraft, and so good is this in the European environment that A-10A pilots have said that accompanying aircraft on a training sortie have been difficult to spot.

Fairchild Republic's other major program involves the projected replacement aircraft for the USAF's Cessna T-37 side-by-side primary jet trainer.

This is known as the NGT (new generation trainer) but carries the Air Force designation T-46A. Expected to appear in prototype form in 1985, it is also a side-by-side two seater but has shoulder-mounted wings and a twin fin and rudder tail unit. Power will be provided by two Garrett turbofan engines. An export version of the T-46A is also being offered as a pilot and weapons trainer under the company designation FRC 225.

During the 1960s Lockheed achieved a major selling success by getting several European air forces to accept into service the F-104G multi-mission version of its Starfighter. When, in the early 1970s, four Starfighter operators (Belgium, the Netherlands, Denmark and Norway) began looking for a replacement, the contenders from European aircraft manufacturers (the Saab Viggen and Dassault-Mirage F1-E) were beaten by the F-16 Fighting Falcon from the USA, partly by the offer of attractive purchasing agreements. As for the much earlier Starfighter program, assembly of European F-16s was allowed to take place in Europe itself. But, unlike the Starfighter, the F-16 has also achieved very great success in attracting orders for the USAF.

The General Dynamics F-16 was originally designed as a small and lightweight day fighter for non-adverse weather use. The first YF-16 took to the air for its maiden flight on 2 February 1974 and, following evaluation against the Northrop YF-17, the type was selected for possible USAF service. As development of the F-16 continued so its capabilities were extended by official requirement, by the installation of radar, all-weather navigation and other avionics and equipment. Its limiting air superiority only role was also in-

creased to take in ground attack. Now the heavier, much more expensive but more versatile F-16 was ready for production in F-16A single-seat and F-16B two-seat training versions. European F-16s were similarly effected, which in the event made more sense for a new combat aircraft that was to operate in the unpredictable weather conditions of Europe.

F-16s began entering service with the USAF and the air forces of Belgium and the Netherlands in 1979, followed in early 1980 by the first of those for the other two European nations. F-16 production in the USA and Europe has totaled more than 1100, examples having also been delivered to Israel and Egypt, Pakistan and Venezuela. It is anticipated that the USAF will eventually receive 2165 F-16s, built over many years. Some of these will be used to update the equipment of the Air Force Reserve and Air National Guard, deliveries to which have begun. South Korea is also a future operator of the F-16.

F-16s being built to later orders are designated F-16C and D for the single- and two-seater versions respectively. The new designations imply aircraft that incorporate provision for new systems to ensure them combat efficiency in the future. The first of these entered service in 1984. A further USAF designation, that of F-16E, applies to the General Dynamic's-conceived F-16XL, a very modified version of the Fighting Falcon with so-called 'cranked arrow' delta-type wings. It is intended to rival the McDonnell Douglas Enhanced Eagle for possible USAF orders for a new combat plane with improved interdiction and air defense capabilities. Both the F-16E and Enhanced Eagle are basically private venture

developments which may not attract orders. Compared to the standard F-16A, the F-16E has improved take-off performance and longer range, and is capable of carrying weapons on a greater number of wing and under-fuselage stations.

The basic F-16A is powered by a single Pratt & Whitney F100-PW-200 turbofan, fed with air via a large intake under the fuselage. Its airframe is otherwise conventional. It has a maximum speed in excess of Mach 2 and a combat radius of more than 925km

Inset: The tandem cockpit arrangement of the F-16B is clearly visible from this Israeli-operated aircraft.

(575 miles). Armament comprises a fixed 20mm multi-barrel cannon plus six Sidewinder air-to-air missiles or a variety of ground attack weapons and auxiliary fuel drop-tanks up to a maximum weight of 9276kg (20,450lb). This incredible stores carrying capability for an aircraft weighing only 16,057kg (35,400lb) in attack configuration is greater than can be claimed for most non-lightweight combat fighters.

Above: One of the 24 F-16s delivered to the Venezuelan Air Force from 1983.

Inset: The F-16XL featuring newly developed 'cranked arrow' delta-type wings to improve performance and increase the number of weapons that can be carried.

To General Dynamics, breaking new ground is nothing new. Way back in December 1964 the company flew the prototype of what was to become the world's first operational variable-geometry (swing-wing) aircraft, in the form of the F-111 two-seat tactical fighter-bomber. Although it cannot be claimed that the F-111 is among the most modern aircraft in terms of recent production, as this was undertaken between the early 1960s and 1976, it will remain a vital part of the USAF and Royal Australian Air Force for many years to come.

The initial production version was the F-111A, which entered USAF service in 1967. This proved to be the major variant, accounting for 141 of the 437 full-production aircraft for the USAF. Each F-111A is powered by two Pratt & Whitney TF30-P-3 turbofan engines, allowing a maximum speed of

Top: The final production version of the General Dynamics F-111 was the F-111F, the only version capable of the full Mach 2.5 originally specified.

Left: The General Dynamics FB-111A is the USAF's only supersonic strategic bomber.

Below: The EF-111A is an electronic countermeasures tactical jamming conversion of the F-111A, distinguished by its tailfin avionics pod.

Right: The missile options for the F-14 Tomcat include Sparrows and Sidewinders, as seen here.

Mach 2.2. Range is more than 5090km (3165 miles). Weapons carried in the fuselage bay and underwing can include conventional or nuclear types. The final fighter-bomber version was the F-111F, the only version to achieve the Mach 2.5 maximum speed specified in the original USAF requirement. In addition, the RAAF received 24 F-111Cs, which in recent years have been supplemented by a small number of ex-USAF F-111As to make good attrition.

A development of the F-111 as a two-seat strategic bomber became the FB-111A. Although the USAF had a planned requirement for 253, it received only 76 by 1971. Capable of the full Mach 2.5 performance and a range in excess of 6440km (4000 miles), it took over the role of supersonic bomber from the delta-winged Convair B-58 Hustler and thereafter supplemented the USAF's B-52 bomber force. Those FB-111As still in use are equipped to carry six SRAM nuclear short range attack missiles or up to 14,288kg (31,500lb) of conventional weapons.

Also important is the USAF's EF-111A electronic countermeasures tactical Jamming conversions of the F-111A. The USAF plans to operate 42. This scale of conversion will leave only 44 F-111As in operational service.

Conversion of the F-111A to EF-111A configuration is undertaken by the Grumman Aerospace Corporation, whose own products in the jet aircraft field are widely operated by the US Navy. Indeed, this company's tradition of equipping the Navy with combat planes goes back to before the Second World War, its wartime piston-engined fighters and bombers including the famous and outstanding F4F Wildcat, F6F Hellcat and TBF Avenger.

Continuing another Grumman tradition of naming its fighters in 'cat' series, when the US Navy required a new multi-role fighter to replace F-4 Phantom IIs on board aircraft carriers, it came up with the tandem two-seat and variable-geometry F-14 Tomcat. The first prototype F-14 took to the air for its initial flight on 21 December

1970. Carrier trials began in 1972 and later the same year two squadrons were declared operational. Today there are more than twenty F-14 squadrons in the US Navy and production will continue at a low rate into the next decade. Iran also received 80 during the 1970s but it is not clear how many are still serviceable.

Very much in the 'heavy' fighter class, the Tomcat is capable of Mach 2.34 on the power of its two Pratt & Whitney TF30-P-412A or later TF30-P-414A turbofan engines. Like many of the world's latest combat aircraft, the F-14 uses a twin tail unit. In a fighter role, armament comprises a combination of Sparrow, Sidewinder and Phoenix air-to-air missiles. This last type had been developed originally to arm the planned US Navy variant of the F-111, which was canceled. Up to six Phoenix can be carried at a time, each with a range of 200km (124 miles), and the Tomcat is capable of tracking multiple targets and attacking them simultaneously.

In a different vein, Grumman is currently constructing a demonstrator fighter for the USAF as the X-29A. This has forward-swept wings which are expected to offer many advantages for small and light tactical fighters, including better maneuverability and low speed flight characteristics. Other Grumman jets to be found on board US Navy aircraft carriers are the A-6 Intruder low-level attack bomber and derivatives known as the KA-6D refueling tanker and EA-6A and EA-6B Prowler tactical ECM aircraft. The EA-6s were developed to suppress enemy electronics and collect electronic intelligence. The Intruder first appeared in 1960 and the A-6A initial production version was delivered to the US Navy from 1963. Several versions followed, leading to the latest A-6E. This model will remain in production for a few more years, despite its initial deployment with the Navy in 1972. The latest off the production line are known as A-6E/TRAMs, indicating the carriage of new electronic equipment to enhance the detection of targets in all weather conditions and the ability to attack them more precisely using standard or laser guided weapons. Earlier built A-6Es are also being updated to this standard.

The Intruder itself is a two-seater, powered by two Pratt & Whitney J52-P-8B turbojet engines installed in the forward fuselage beneath the wing roots. It has a maximum speed of 1037km/h (644mph) and a range, according to the fuel and weapon load carried, of 1627–5220km (1010–3245 miles). The heavy weapon load, weighing up to 8165kg (18,000lb) but usually lower to make allowance for auxiliary fuel tanks to extend range, can be conventional or nuclear and has recently been expanded to include the Harpoon anti-shipping missile.

In 1959 the Northrop Corporation's new small and lightweight F-5 tactical fighter appeared on the aviation scene. Intended for export to nations not requiring the type of heavy and very fast combat aircraft typified by those designed for USAF service, the single-seat F-5A, which could achieve Mach 1.4, and its slightly slower tandem two-seat training variant, the F-5B, found favor with a great many air forces around the world.

As a more modern aircraft to supersede the original F-5s, Northrop developed the similar looking Tiger II, offered in F-5E single-seat and F5F two-seat training forms. Apart from the small numbers that joined the USAF and US Navy in training roles from 1973 – their functions including making surprise mock attacks on operational squadrons in an 'aggressor' training role and use at training schools at home and in the Philippines and the UK – these too have been widely deployed by foreign air forces. Tiger IIs bring the total number of countries that have ordered/received F-5 series aircraft to more than 30, including such unlikely users as Vietnam.

The F-5E has a higher maximum speed than the F-5A, achieving Mach 1.64 on the power of two General Electric J85-GE-21B turbojet engines. It is also more maneuverable. In an air-to-air role the usual armament is the two fixed 20mm cannon plus two Sidewinder missiles. For attack, the 3175kg (7000lb) maximum external load can include a wide variety of bombs, rocket packs and missiles. Carrying Sidewinders and its maximum fuel load, the F-5E has an operational radius of 1056km (656 miles). An armed reconnaissance version of the F-5E is also available as the RF-5E Tigereye, which has attracted orders from Malaysia and Saudi Arabia, which are already F-5 users.

On 30 August 1982 Northrop flew the prototype of a further development of the F-5, then known as the F-5G. Since redesignated F-20 Tigershark, it also is intended for export but can demonstrate a maximum speed in excess of Mach 2 and the very high rate of climb of 16,000m (52,800ft) per min. This is achieved mainly by the adoption of a

Left: Due to be flight tested in 1984, the first of two Grumman X-29A technology demonstrators is seen during construction with the forward-swept wings mated to the fuselage.

Below: A Grumman EA-6B Prowler of Navy squadron VAQ-129.

Previous pages, inset: The Brazilian Air Force is one operator of the Northrop F-5E Tiger II light tactical fighter, this aircraft carrying wingtip-mounted Sidewinders.

Previous pages: America's newest fighter is the Northrop F-20 Tigershark, the prototype of which is seen here streaking over the desert during a mock sortie in California.

Right: Currently in widespread service with the US Air National Guard is the Vought A-7D Corsair II single-seat close air support and interdiction aircraft.

Below: A single-seat A-7E and two-seat TA-7C of Navy squadron VA-122 from USS *Lexington.*

single General Electric F404-GE-100 turbofan engine, which offers very much more thrust than the F-5E's two engines together, at an acceptable increase in gross weight. Bahrain is likely to be the first customer for the Tigershark, an aircraft which proved one of the main attractions of the 1983 Paris Air Show.

Northrop also has available its F/A-18L. This is basically a land-based strike fighter variant of the McDonnell Douglas Hornet, both aircraft having been derived from the lightweight YF-17 prototype and both programs involving the two companies either as prime or main subcontractor. The F/A-18L, which has a similar engine to the Hornet, is considerably lighter as it has no need to carry the naval equipment that makes the Hornet suited to aircraft carrier operations. Indeed, it has a maximum speed of about Mach 2 and can offer either an increased weapon carrying capability or longer range. The fact that the F/A-18L has not been selected so far for service abroad, orders instead having gone to the Hornet, must in some part reflect the hidden advantages of purchasing an aircraft type that is in high-volume production for the US forces. Certainly the F/A-18L was evaluated by the Spanish Air Force, which has Hornets on order. Both types are, nevertheless, basically similar and very fine combat aircraft.

The Vought Corporation is a subsidiary of The LTV Corporation, the latter of which was formed from earlier companies that enjoyed a long tradition of designing and producing aircraft for the US Navy. The most recent Vought naval aircraft is the A-7 Corsair II, which was designed as a relatively inexpensive, subsonic, light attack aircraft for deployment on aircraft carriers. Its design was based on the company's earlier Crusader naval fighter.

Production of the single-seat Corsair II began in the 1960s with the A-7A. More recent versions have included the A-7D, of which more than 450 were completed for the USAF up to 1976. This version is currently in widespread use with the Air National Guard. The most recent US Navy version has been the A-7E, of which nearly 600 had been delivered by the close of production in 1981. Powered by an Allison TF41-A-2 turbofan engine (a version of the Rolls-Royce Spey specially developed by Allison and the British engine company to power the latest versions of the Corsair II), the A-7E has a maximum speed of 1112km/h (691mph) and a range with maximum standard fuel of 3670km (2281 miles) for long distance

non-combat flights. It can carry up to 6805kg (15,000lb) of weapons and other external stores, in addition to a standard 20mm cannon.

A version of the A-7E for service as a land-based attack aircraft with the Hellenic Air Force is the A-7H, and Greece has also received a small number of TA-7H two-seat trainers. Portugal has also recently upgraded its air force with the deployment of A-7Ps, representing refurbished and modernized A-7As.

Although the US Navy is receiving Hornets partly as Corair II replacements, the A-7 will remain an important

attack aircraft in international service for some years to come. Reflecting the importance of the A-7D version to ANG units, Vought has produced, in the 1980s, a small number of new and longer two-seat combat-capable trainers as A-7Ks for operation by these units.

Of course the development of new military and civil aircraft in the USA continues, as in other major aircraft producing countries, and already the first details are coming to light of futuristic aircraft, some of which are not planned for service until the next century.

Despite the political shifts of 1960 that resulted in the breakdown of close relations between China and the Soviet Union, it is a curious fact that China's presentday aircraft industry is, more than two decades later, still reliant in part on many designs that originated across the border. A clear example of this can be found in the production of the J-6, a Chinese version of the Mikoyan MiG-19 (NATO name *Farmer*). This entered service in its original Chinese Jianjiji-6 form as a cannon-armed day fighter with the Air Force of the People's Liberation Army in 1962 and was still in production in its latest forms (and for export as the F-6) in the early 1980s at the Tianjin and Shenyang factories. Other examples are the J-7, a version of the Mikoyan MiG-21 (NATO name *Fishbed-C*) produced at Xian; the H-5, a designation relating to the Ilyushin Il-28 light tactical bomber (NATO name *Beagle*) produced at Harbin; and the H-6, a Chinese version of the Tupolev Tu-16 (NATO name *Badger*) in production at Xian. These do not take account of non-jet aircraft, such as the Chinese version of the Mil Mi-4 and Mi-8 helicopters, and various radial- and turbo-prop-powered transports and trainers.

The only transport aircraft in current operation able to demonstrate the benefits that arise from two above-wing turbofan engines is the Soviet Antonov An-72.

Above: Chinese-built Shenyang J-6 fighter photographed at night.

Add to these Chinese developed two-seat derivatives of single-seat jets, such as the JJ-5 training variant of the J-5/MiG-17 and the JJ-6 trainer based on the J-6, and the picture becomes clear.

Yet the above also gives an in-accurate view of the Chinese aircraft industry, which has also been respon-sible in recent years for developing its own aircraft for military and civil use. The production of Soviet-originated aircraft after 1960 stems almost en-tirely from steps taken before this date to set up production lines for these aircraft in China with Soviet assist-ance. Thereafter the Chinese industry had to go it alone. It is a tribute to the Soviet designs that China has con-sidered most of them worthy of long production runs.

The J-6 has a maximum speed without external stores of Mach 1.45 and can be armed with Chinese-developed CAA-1 infra-red homing air-to-air or Chinese-built early type Sidewinder missiles, rockets or bombs. Power is provided by two Wopen-6 turbojet engines, evolved from the Soviet Tumansky R-9BF-811 type. It appears that the MiG-21 was not as popular in China as elsewhere

in the world, as production of the J-7 has been limited.

A Chinese originated combat air-craft, capable of ground attack and close air support but also deployed by the Navy as a fighter, is the Qianhjiji-5 or Q-5. This is known to NATO by the name *Fantan-A* and has also been exported to Pakistan as the A-5. Al-though based on the J-6 and powered by similar engines, it has a longer fuselage to accommodate a greatly increased fuel load, a so-called 'solid' nose containing radar, and side air intakes. The avionics for the Q-5 are almost certainly to a higher standard. Armament, in addition to the fixed 23mm cannon, comprises up to 2000kg (4409lb) of ground attack missiles, bombs or rockets, or a tactical nuclear weapon. In an air-to-air role armament is CAA-2s, Chinese-built Sidewinders or Matra R.550 Magic missiles. The Q-5 is known to be supersonic and to have an operating radius with a full attack weapon load of about 600km (373 miles).

The subject of much speculation is the latest Chinese combat aircraft, the J-8, which has been given the name *Finback* by NATO. This is a Mach 2 fighter of advanced design that has been under development at Shenyang for a decade. A prototype was seen by an American delegation in 1980 and it

is now known that it has a French modern Mirage-type configuration with delta wings and a fin and rudder tail unit only. However, it is uncertain whether the J-8 has, as yet, entered production.

Probably a little before work began on the J-8 at Shenyang, a project was initiated at Shanghai that culminated, on 26 September 1980, with the first flight of a Chinese designed and built large commercial jet airliner. Known as the Yunshuji-10 or Y-10, it is a 124- to 178-passenger transport powered by four Pratt & Whitney JT3D-7 turbofan engines carried on pylons under the well swept-back wings. Three proto-types have been built but it is thought that a production decision is still to be made. It could also have the type of military applications found in the US for the Boeing 707. Maximum cruising speed has been quoted at 974km/h (605mph), and range with a full load at 5560km (3454 miles).

Despite Chinese production of the J-7 having been surprisingly limited, the Soviet Mikoyan MiG-21 itself has proved to be the world's most used fighter and until a few years ago was the main Soviet tactical fighter. More recently, however, this role has been assumed by the variable-geometry MiG-23/27.

The MiG-21 first flew as a prototype

in the Soviet Union in mid-1956 as a single-turbojet, small and light, very maneuverable and fast climbing fighter to supersede the MiG-19, from which it was very differently configured. It also represents Mikoyan's only production fighter of tailed-delta type. The first major version was the MiG-21F, known to NATO by the name *Fishbed-C* and the aircraft upon which China based its J-7. This was the ultimate development of the first-generation MiG-21, still basically a day fighter with limited avionics but armed with K-13 (NATO *Atoll*) air-to-air missiles or rockets in addition to cannon.

Second-generation MiG-21s began with the -21PF (NATO *Fishbed-D*), a much improved aircraft with better range, more power and the necessary improvements in avionics for all-weather use. Many other variants have followed these for operation by the air forces of many nations, including recon-naissance and tandem two-seat train-ing models. The MiG-21 in its penulti-mate form is typified by the MiG-21MF (*Fishbed-J*), which was delivered from 1970. Armed with a 23mm twin-barrel cannon and four *Atoll/Advanced Atoll* missiles or rockets and bombs, it is capable of a maximum speed of Mach 2.1 on the power of its single Tumansky R-13-300 turbojet. Indeed, in the past western observers often pointed to Soviet engines as a weakness, stating that they had to be changed too fre-quently to allow an air force to main-tain high serviceability of aircraft in an emergency. This can no longer be said, with the latest MiG-21s capable of performing many missions a day over a crisis period and with an engine change required only after several hundred hours.

The ultimate MiG-21 is the -21*bis*, known to NATO as *Fishbed-N*. A third and final generation aircraft with im-proved avionics, it is the most powerful thanks to its Tumansky R-25 turbojet and has the extremely high rate of climb of about 17,700m (58,070ft) per minute. It carries the highly maneuver-able close-range *Aphid* dogfight mis-siles in addition to *Atolls*. This is one version of the MiG-21 also to have been produced in India, while an earlier manufacturing country (under license) of the MiG-21 was Czechoslovakia.

Without doubt the most important small Soviet aircraft in production today is the Mikoyan MiG-23 variable-geometry (swing-wing) fighter and its ground attack counterpart, the MiG-27. Yearly production of these aircraft alone in the Soviet Union is almost certainly greater than the combined US production of the F-14, F-15, F-16 and F/A-18. *Flogger*, to give them their combined NATO reporting name, has taken over as the Soviet air forces' most important tactical aircraft and deploy-

Above: Four Q-5s of the Air Force of the People's Liberation Army photographed during a training sortie, each carrying two under-wing 760-liter drop-tanks.

Left: Egyptian Air Force-operated Mikoyan MiG-21R, a tactical reconnaissance aircraft seen here with an underfuselage reconnaissance pack.

ment is almost certainly approaching 3000. MiG-23/-27s have also been ex-ported to Warsaw Pact and other nations.

The prototype MiG-23 appeared in about 1967 but large numbers of pro-duction aircraft did not begin to enter Soviet units until 1973. By far the most important version is the MiG-23MF, which has been identified in two sub-variants that are known to NATO as *Flogger-B* and *Flogger-G*. These are used as interceptors by Voyska PVO, the Soviet Air Defense Command force, and as tactical aircraft by units of Frontal Aviation (Frontovaya Aviasiya). *Flogger-B* has a maximum speed of Mach 2.35 on the power of its single Tumansky R-29 turbojet engine or can fly supersonically at sea level. Its one 23mm twin-barrel cannon is supplemented by six air-to-air missiles of *Aphid* and long-range *Apex* types or ground attack weapons. Its operational radius of action can be up to 1300km (808 miles), although normally less. The similar *Flogger-G* introduced several changes, including a lighter radar that retains the ability to track aircraft flying at lower altitudes. Export examples are the *Flogger-E* interceptor and *Flogger-F* and *-H* attack aircraft.

The export attack aircraft mentioned above are the only versions of the MiG-23 to incorporate the redesigned sloping nose that typifies the MiG-27, indicating the removal of an interceptor-type search radar but the adoption of a laser rangefinder. True MiG-27s also have fixed air intakes and engine nozzles, suited to aircraft expected to operate at transonic speeds at low level, plus a 23mm six-barrel gun which is more appropriate than the interceptor's twin-barrel GSh-23. Two versions of the MiG-27 have been identified, the *Flogger-D* original model

capable of a 3000kg (6614lb) weapon load and the later *Flogger-J* with armament that includes two gun pods carried under the wings. Although the weapon carrying capability appears light by western aircraft standards, MiG-27s (like earlier Sukhoi Su-7Bs) are among the aircraft assigned to carry tactical nuclear weapons as alternatives to conventional loads and therefore require no extra carrying capability. Maximum speed on the power of the lower thrust R-29B engine is Mach 1.7 at high altitude and more than Mach 1 at sea level.

In the mid-1960s work broke of a new Soviet interceptor that was suggested to be by far the most advanced in the world. A record-breaking example of this aircraft indicated that a production version could have extremely high speed, and indeed the MiG-25, known to NATO and the western public as *Foxbat*, can achieve a remarkable Mach 3.2. This is a far greater speed than can be attained by any western interceptor.

The original *Foxbat-A* single-seat interceptor was quickly joined by the *Foxbat-B* high-speed reconnaissance variant, then by the MiG-25U tandem cockpit trainer (*Foxbat-C*) and finally by an improved reconnaissance version as the *Foxbat-D*. The mystery surrounding the *Foxbat* was heightened in the early 1970s, at a time when probably only the A and B versions of *Foxbat* had been deployed, when a small number of Soviet aircraft stationed in Egypt undertook reconnaissance missions off Israel. Phantom IIs scrambled to intercept them failed in their mission. However, in 1976 a *Foxbat* was flown to Japan by a defecting Soviet pilot, which allowed the west a chance of proper assessment.

Left: The Mikoyan MiG-23MF *Flogger-G* **is one of the versions of the MiG-23 variable-geometry combat aircraft to serve as an interceptor and tactical fighter with the Soviet forces.**

Above left: The Mikoyan MiG-25 *Foxbat* **in interceptor form is finding a new role with the Soviet Voyska PVO, to combat low-flying cruise missiles.**

Above: Sweeping fast overhead is a *Foxbat-A* **operated by the Libyan Air Force, armed with two large** *Acrid* **air-to-air missiles.**

Foxbat had been originally conceived to intercept the North American B-70 Valkyrie Mach 3 cruise bomber that was under development for the USAF. This bomber was canceled in 1961, but the potential of the MiG was seen as so great that its development program was continued, taking in as equally important a reconnaissance role. The *Foxbat* flown under Japanese radar defenses to land at Hakodate airport in 1976 was not particularly well equipped and was judged to have an unnecessarily heavy airframe. Its high speed resulted from two large Tumansky R-31 turbojet engines carried in the rear fuselage beneath the twin tailfins, but Mach 2.83 was the maximum speed for the aircraft while armed with air-to-air missiles. However, a number of very ingenious ideas

were incorporated into the design and the airborne computer was particularly fine. The latter would allow the interceptor to be guided automatically to its target by a controlling ground defense system.

The exact production total of MiG-25 interceptors is unknown but it is likely to have been well over 400. Their initial low acceleration rates are made up for by much improved acceleration later and a very high service ceiling. However, as the *Foxbat-A* was designed mainly to counter a high-speed and high-altitude bomber threat that never materialized, a large number of these have been undergoing conversion to make them suitable to intercept very low-flying cruise missiles of the type selected for deployment by NATO. These converted and possibly more powerful interceptors are *Foxbat-E*s. Armament for *Foxbat-A*, and presumably *Foxbat-E*, is a combination of four *Acrid*, *Apex* and *Aphid* air-to-air missiles. *Foxbats* also serve with the air forces of Algeria, Libya, India and Syria.

In 1983 the Soviet Union began operational use of a new interceptor that has almost certainly been developed to counter NATO cruise missiles and low altitude penetration bom-

bers of the future B-1B type. Based on the MiG-25 but probably longer and with many airframe refinements and much improved avionics, it is likely to have *Foxbat-E*'s more-powerful engines. For its main lower altitude role, the two-seat MiG-31, known to NATO as *Foxhound*, probably has a maximum speed of about Mach 2.4 and much better performance at this altitude than *Foxbat*. Armament, in addition of a cannon, is most likely to be eight new air-to-air missiles known as AA-9s, which would suit *Foxhound*'s ability to detect and engage targets flying at much lower altitude.

Even less is known of the Mikoyan MiG-29 (NATO *Fulcrum*), which is currently under test and could be operational with the Soviet forces as a single-seat all-weather fighter and attack aircraft by about 1985. A twin-engined, twin vertical tail combat plane, it is probably similar in configuration to the US Hornet but with higher performance. It is almost certain to be capable of carrying AA-9s as a missile option.

Another new Soviet fighter currently being tested at Ramenskoye has been credited to Sukhoi and given the type number and NATO name Su-27 and *Flanker* respectively by the west.

Left: One of the nations to receive the Sukhoi Su-20 (*Fitter-C*) was Egypt, a less well-equipped export version of the Su-17 variable-geometry attack fighter.

Thought to be larger than *Fulcrum*, in fact in the class of the USAF's F-15 Eagle, if it goes into service it is likely to be at least as combat capable as the US type, with a secondary attack role.

Sukhoi jets currently operational include the Su-7B ground attack aircraft (NATO named *Fitter-A*), which dates from the 1950s and certainly cannot be termed a modern type. Su-7Bs are virtually out of service with the Soviet forces but continue to be important to the air forces of other nations. The Su-15 is another Sukhoi that is very gradually being superseded, although in this case about 700 are still thought to remain operational within the Voyska PVO's current force of 2250 air defense interceptors. Known to NATO by the reporting name *Flagon*, its continuing role in protecting Soviet airspace was brought to world attention in 1983 when the type intercepted a Korean Air Lines Boeing 747-200. When armed with four air-to-air missiles and cannon, this single-seat all-weather interceptor can achieve a speed of Mach 2.3 on the power of two turbojet engines.

To supersede the Su-7, Sukhoi clearly decided that an update of the earlier attack aircraft would be sufficient to achieve the required performance goals. This view, if correct, is not altogether surprising, as the Su-7 had proven a very willing workhorse. Therefore, when in the early 1970s units of the Soviet tactical air forces began deploying the new aircraft as the Su-17 (NATO named *Fitter-C*), it was seen in the west to be basically an Su-7 fuselage married to new wings with variable-geometry outer sections. It was to take some years for those outside the Soviet Union to fully understand the improvements incorporated into the Su-17. For

a start the newly fitted Lyulka turbojet engine offered more power and the avionics were much improved. All the updates in the Su-17 meant that it was capable of achieving Mach 2.17 at high altitude and more than Mach 1 at sea level, could carry a 4000kg (8818lb) payload of conventional or tactical nuclear weapons instead of the former 2500kg (5510lb), had a longer range and needed a shorter distance to take off when operating from unprepared fields or airstrips. As a consequence, many hundreds of Su-17s are operated by the Soviet Union (including some for naval strike duties), in *Fitter-C* and subsequent variants. Reduced standard but similar Su-20s have been exported, together with exported and more powerful Su-22s. However, the latter possess, probably, the lowest standard of avionics and equipment of any modern *Fitter* variant.

Not exported is the Sukhoi Su-24, a two-seat Mach 2+ variable-geometry attack aircraft that is very much the Soviet equivalent of the USAF's F-111. *Fencer*, to give it its NATO name, has been in service for a little over a decade and is undoubtedly still in production even though probably about 600 are already deployed by tactical units. Power is provided by two Lyulka turbojet engines and it has the capability of carrying up to about 8000kg (17,637lb) of conventional or nuclear weapons. It also has advanced avionic systems, including terrain avoidance radar for use during high-speed, low-level attack missions.

America can be said to have influenced another type of Soviet aircraft, the Sukhoi Su-25. This is a subsonic fixed-wing ground attack aircraft, very much in the mold of the USAF's A-10A Thunderbolt although

somewhat different in configuration. It is thought to have two turbojet engines installed under the roots of the very long and slightly swept shoulder-mounted wings. Unexpectedly, the pilot occupies a cockpit more suited to a fighter than a ground attack aircraft, with vision limited to ahead and sideways. Like the Thunderbolt, the Su-25's main weapon is a heavy multi-barrel cannon, although all manner of other weapons can be carried on pylons. Given the reporting name *Frogfoot* by NATO, the aircraft has seen action in Afghanistan, where it has partnered the Mil Mi-24 *Hind* heavily armed assault helicopter. However, full deployment has only just begun in the Soviet tactical forces. It is almost certain to take up positions with the *Hind* in forward areas of Europe and elsewhere. Maximum speed could be about 880km/h (547mph) and a radius of action of 556km (345 miles) has been quoted.

Antonov has been most readily associated, for a very long time, with the long-serving An-2 biplane and a number of large and small turboprop-powered transports. Its two latest transports have broken this mold, however, with both the An-72 and An-400 using turbofan power.

The An-72 (NATO *Coaler*) is a new light STOL (short take-off and landing) transport that first appeared as a prototype at the end of 1977. It is expected to be seen in production form at any moment for Aeroflot and military use. Like the abandoned American Boeing YC-14 of 1976, it has two turbofan engines (in this case Lotarev D-36s) mounted above the relatively small-span wings and a rear fuselage door/ramp for straight-in loading of freight, vehicles or other items of equipment. Folding side-wall seats are fitted for 32 persons. The engine arrangement has several advantages over conventional configurations, including giving a low infra-red signature to an enemy's ground detection systems and a lower noise footprint, and offers improved thrust reversal. It also gives an unobstructed area below the high-mounted wings for ease of freight handling, and allows the opportunity of carrying underwing stores if required. Designed as a replacement for the An-26, it has a maximum payload capacity of 10,000kg (22,046lb), a cruising speed of 720km/h (447mph) and a range varying between 1000 and 3800km (621 and 2361 miles) according to the payload/fuel carried.

Although not expected to be seen in

military or civil use until the second half of this decade, the An-400 is of particular interest. It is the new Soviet very heavy and long-range strategic transport to supersede the turboprop-powered An-22 and is thought to be even larger than the USAF's C-5 Galaxy. If this is indeed correct, the An-400 is the world's largest operational aircraft. Like the Galaxy, it is powered by four large turbofan engines (probably Kuznetsovs) and could carry a payload of 120,000kg (264,554lb) over a distance of 4600km (2858 miles).

In 1963 the first flight took place of a new Soviet four-engined long-range airliner which entered production for Aeroflot and several other airlines as the Ilyushin Il-62 (NATO *Classic*). Production examples were given Kuznetsov NK-8-4 turbofan engines, mounted, British VC10 fashion, in pairs on the rear fuselage. The basic Il-62 remains in use today. However, in the 1970s new versions appeared as the Il-62M and later Il-62MK, accommodating 140 to 174 passengers. Maximum normal cruising speed is 900km/h (559mph) and range with a full load is 7800km (4847 miles).

Below: The Su-22 (*Fitter-J*) is another export version of the Su-17 *Fitter-C*. This aircraft serves with the Libyan air force.

Inset: Ilyushin Il-62M in Aeroflot markings, seen at London's Heathrow Airport.

Below: The Soviet Union's first wide-bodied airliner is the Ilyushin Il-86, seen here at the 1981 Paris Air Show.

ventional missiles or bombs, and also serves in a maritime role, is the Tupolev Tu-22 (NATO *Blinder*). The Tu-22 appeared as a prototype in the early 1960s and was the first Soviet supersonic bomber. It is powered by two turbojet engines, one each side of the vertical tail, and has an estimated maximum speed of Mach 1.4. Libya and Iraq both operate ex-Soviet *Blinders* in conventionally armed roles.

Supersonic performance and longer range appear to have been the main aims for the latest Soviet bombers, and the Long-Range Air Force (Aviatsiya Dalnyevo Deistviya) has today by far the most formidable bomber force in the world. Tupolev is responsible for two new supersonic bombers, the widely deployed Tu-22M (NATO *Backfire*) and a new aircraft that is expected to become operational in about 1986 and which is known only in the west by its NATO allocated name *Blackjack*. The

Above left: The huge Myasishchev M-4 (NATO *Bison*) is still operated by the Soviet forces as a strategic bomber, an in-flight refueling tanker, and as a maritime reconnaissance aircraft.

Left: A Soviet-operated Tupolev Tu-22 *Blinder*, that nation's first supersonic bomber.

Below: The only large supersonic bomber in service today, and the only large bomber with variable-geometry wings, is the Soviet Mach 2+ Tupolev Tu-22M *Backfire*. This example of a *Backfire-B* was photographed by an aircraft from the Swedish Air Force.

A very different Ilyushin transport is the Il-76 (NATO *Candid*), intended as an Antonov An-12 replacement and capable of transporting a payload of 40,000kg (88,184lb) over a range of 5000km (3107 miles). First flown in 1971, several versions have entered service with Aeroflot and other airlines, while military examples with tail guns are used by Soviet Military Transport Aviation (Aviatsiya Vozdushno-Dessantnikh Voisk) as troop (140) and freight transports and by other air forces. Future military variants include a flight refueling tanker for Soviet supersonic bombers and an AWACS version known already to NATO as *Mainstay*. It is entirely possible that the first *Mainstays* are already in squadron use, offering much improved capabilities over the earlier Tu-126 *Moss* AWACS type.

In December 1980 and July 1981 Aeroflot inaugurated scheduled domestic and international services respectively with the Ilyushin Il-86 (NATO *Camber*), the Soviet Union's first widebodied passenger airliner. This accommodates up to 350 passengers and has a configuration not unlike a European Airbus A300 fuselage fitted with Boeing

747 wings and engines. Of course this description bears no relationship to the actual design, which has a fuselage about 6m (20ft) longer than the A300 and a wing span very much shorter than the 747. Power is provided by four Kuznetsov NK-86 turbofan engines, which allow a cruising speed of 950km/h (590mph) and a maximum range of about 4600km (2860 miles). A longer-range derivative of the Il-86 is thought to exist as the Il-96.

Old style jet bombers still in use with Soviet strategic forces include the huge Myasishchev M-4 (NATO *Bison*) and the medium-range Tupolev Tu-16 (NATO *Badger*). Both of these aircraft types are also operated in flight refueling tanker versions to extend the endurance of the turboprop-powered Tu-95 *Bear* and modern supersonic strategic bomber forces, whilst *Badgers* also undertake important maritime and electronic roles. Maximum speed of *Badger*, powered by two Mikulin AM-3 turbojet engines, is about 992km/h (616mph) and its conventional or nuclear bombload can weigh 9000kg (19,840lb). Egypt also operates *Badgers*.

Another older type Soviet bomber that carries long-range nuclear/con-

latter bomber is known to have been under test at Ramenskoye in the early 1980s. Satellite photos have shown this bomber on the ground and flying alongside Tupolev Tu-144 supersonic airliners, which undoubtedly assisted in the flight testing program. Earlier suggestions that the Tu-144 itself had formed the basis of an abandoned experimental strategic bomber prototype have now been generally dismissed.

Like *Backfire*, *Blackjack* is a variable-geometry bomber of very advanced design. It is thought to be capable of an operating radius of 7300km (4536 miles) without having to take on fuel from an airborne tanker aircraft. With inflight refueling this range would be greatly increased, making any target within its scope. Moreover, it appears that it has a maximum speed of more than Mach 2, therefore making it much faster than the USAF's projected B-1B. Reports suggest that it is larger than the B-1B and B-52 but capable of carrying a smaller warload. The lower payload-carrying capability of *Blackjack* should not prove a problem for its operators, especially in the knowledge that one weapon option that might be available is a Soviet-developed long-range air launched cruise missile.

Backfire, as mentioned previously, is currently the world's only large variable-geometry supersonic strategic bomber and has no western equivalent. Well over 200 are already in service with Soviet strategic nuclear forces and the Soviet Naval Air Fleet (for maritime use) and production continues to add new aircraft to the forces at a fairly high rate. It is considered most likely that 400 *Backfires* will represent the optimum force level, with new production making good attrition.

Several versions of *Backfire* have been identified, each as an improvement over previous production aircraft. Each bomber is capable of carrying 12,000kg (26,455lb) of weapons, with *Kitchen* or *Kingfish* (NATO names) nuclear or conventionally armed air-to-surface missiles as its main armament, soon undoubtedly to be supplemented by long-range air-launched cruise missiles. Defensive capability is provided by two 23mm radar-directed cannon in the tail.

Backfire is known to have a maximum speed of Mach 2 and can achieve a very high subsonic speed at low altitude. All examples appear to have the housing for flight refueling, although those recently seen while flying in Europe usually have the actual nose probe removed. Even without refueling *Backfire* can fly about 5475km (3400 miles) from base before returning, making it the most formidable bomber of either Warsaw Pact or NATO forces in Europe, where the majority are based. Others have joined a strategic force in the Pacific area, five of which were recently located by Japanese aircraft while over international water. This deployment has resulted in the USAF decision to replace its conventionally armed B-52s in the area with others capable of carrying nuclear weapons. *Backfires* using inflight refueling are capable of reaching potential long distance targets, including those in the North American continent.

The Soviet Union has had less success in developing a supersonic airliner than supersonic bombers. It is generally believed that plans to fly regular Aeroflot services with the Tupolev Tu-144/-144D have been given up. In most respects, the Tu-144 and European Concorde are very similar.

Tupolev has made a number of major contributions to the world's commercial air transport scene over the years, its earlier products having included the twin-turbofan Tu-134 short- to medium-range airliner accommodating 80 to 90 passengers. However, the Tu-134 is giving way to the Yakovlev Yak 42 with Aeroflot and Aviogenex of Yugoslavia, although it will still be seen for some years to come with Aeroflot and other airlines.

As a medium- to long-range airliner for 128 to 167 passengers, Tupolev produced its Tu-154 (NATO *Careless*). The first Soviet airliner with three rear-mounted engines (Kuznetsov NK-8-2 turbofans), it entered regular passenger services with Aeroflot in early 1972. A developed version that appeared in service two years later is the Tu-154A, with NK-8-2U engines, followed

in 1977 by the refined and improved Tu-154B with accommodation for 154 to 180 passengers. This later version has a normal cruising speed of about 900km/h (559mph) and can fly 2750km (1709 miles) with a full load, a range which can be greatly increased by operating the aircraft with a lighter payload. An all-freight version of the airliner has recently joined the range as the Tu-154C, while a further derivative was being flight tested in the early 1980s as the Tu-164. This most recent development represents a major update of the airliner, incorporating changes to the vertical tail, ailerons and spoilers, and with new Soloviev D-30KU turbofan engines, but accommodating

fewer passengers than the Tu-154B.

Takovlev's three aircraft types that fit into the category of modern jet aircraft are the Yak-36MP (NATO *Forger*), and the Yak-40 short-range and Yak-42 medium-range airliners. As already mentioned, the Yak-42 is replacing the Tu-134 used by Aeroflot and Aviogenex. It is a three-turbofan airliner (Lotarev D-36s) with accommodation for up to 120 passengers and carries the NATO reporting name *Clobber*. The first prototype took to the air initially in March 1975 and in 1980 production aircraft were introduced on Aeroflot's Moscow-Krasnodar service.

The Yak-42's design was based on the bureau's successful but much smaller

Yak-40 (NATO *Codling*), which had been inaugurated into passenger service with Aeroflot in September 1968. This has proven to be one of the most successful Soviet turbine-powered airliners of all time, with more than 800 built. This production figure matches that of the highly acclaimed Ilyushin Il-18. Originally conceived as a modern replacement for the Lisunov Li-2 (the Soviet license-built version of the American Douglas DC-3 that had been flown during and after the Second World War), the Yak-42 can operate from grass airstrips and accommodates between eleven and 32 passengers or freight. Power for this 550km/h (342mph) cruising speed airliner is

Above: One of five Tupolev Tu-134 airliners flown by the Polish airline LOT.

Far right: Balkan Bulgarian Airlines' Tupolev Tu-154B-2 coming in to land at London's Heathrow Airport in March 1983.

Right: The Yakovlev Yak-40 was designed as a modern replacement for the piston-engined Lisunov Li-2 and has proven to be one of the most-produced Soviet airliners ever.

Left: The Yakovlev Yak-42 medium-range airliner was one of the Soviet exhibits at the 1981 Paris Air Show.

provided by three small Ivchenko AI-25 turbofan engines carried at the rear fuselage.

Yakovlev is also world famous for its light training aircraft powered by radial engines and has produced in the past a number of combat planes for the Soviet forces. However, the only Yakovlev combat aircraft that can be termed a modern jet is its Yak-36MP. When first deployed on the Soviet Navy's aircraft carrier *Kiev* in 1976, it became only the second type of operational fixed-wing VTOL (vertical take-off and landing) aircraft anywhere in the world. It has since gone to sea on the *Minsk* and *Novorossiyfk* and will equip one other carrier of this class, but is unlikely to be selected for the new and very large nuclear-powered aircraft carrier believed to be under construction.

Two versions have been seen on board ship, the single-seater known to NATO as *Forger-A* and the two-seat trainer variant (*Forger-B*). Each carrier has about twelve *Forger-A*s and a single *Forger-B* on board, together with a large number of helicopters. Power for the Yak-36MP is provided by a main turbojet engine carried in the center of the fuselage and two far less powerful and smaller liftjets installed vertically in tandem to the rear of the cockpit. The main engine has vectoring nozzles, which face aft for forward flight but are directed slightly forward of vertically-down for VTOL take-offs and landings, during which time the liftjets are used. This power arrangement appears to preclude STOL operations for the *Yak-36MP*, which reduces its possible payload capability. Nevertheless, it can carry a wide variety of attack and air defense weapons up to a maximum of about 1360kg (3000lb) weight. Maximum speed is just subsonic and its radius of action with a full weapon load can be 370km (230 miles). *Yak-36MPs* have not been seen in operational use on land, which might point to the future development of a much modified version of *Forger* or an entirely new V/STOL type.

CHAPTER FIVE

WHERE PARTNERSHIPS ARE MADE

Especially in Europe, but also in other parts of the world, partnerships between governments or manufacturing companies have been established to develop jointly new military and civil aircraft. Not only does such an arrangement help spread the enormous cost of development, which often runs into hundreds of millions of dollars, but can provide the basis for sharing latest technologies or manufacturing benefits. Examples of this are many. The Airbus A300 was developed and is produced by a consortium of companies from West Germany, France, the UK, Spain, the Netherlands and Yugoslavia.

The IAR-93/Orao close support aircraft is the product of Romania and Yugoslavia. Grumman Aerospace in the USA is assisting in the Israeli IAI Lavi program, British Aerospace is collaborating with Saab-Scania of Sweden on part of the Gripen's airframe, and the Soviet-developed Antonov An-28 turboprop-powered transport was entrusted to PZL Mielec of Poland for production. There are many other examples, producing such aircraft as the Alpha Jet trainer, Panavia Tornado and Saab-Fairchild turboprop transport.

Having stated the above, the Alpha Jet, developed jointly by Dassault-

The prototype Dassault-Breguet Mirage III NG that first flew in December 1982, its noticeable external changes including the adoption of foreplanes and a refueling probe.

Above: RAF Hawk T.Mk 1s each carrying rocket launchers.

Above: Some ninety RAF Hawk T.Mk 1 trainers have been equipped to launch AIM-9L Sidewinder air-to-air missiles.

Right: Aermacchi MB.339PANs flown by the Italian Frecce Tricolori aerobatic team.

Below right: Indicating the export success of the Alpha Jet, these three were destined for Qatar (furthest aircraft), the Ivory Coast and Togo (nearest).

Left: First flown in 1980, the Caproni Vizzola C22J is a side-by-side two-seat lightweight trainer powered by two very small Microturbo turbojet engines.

Breguet of France and Dornier of West Germany, is an exception for jet trainers by being an international effort, the market for this type of aircraft having been overwhelmed by national products. Modern jet trainers, intended for basic and advanced instruction and limited combat duties, include the Argentinian FMA IA 63, the Czech Aero L-39 Albatros (although developed with Soviet co-operation), French Microjet 200B, Indian HAL HJT-16 Kiran series, Italian Aermacchi MB.339A, Italian Caproni Vizzola C22J and SIAI-Marchetti S.211, Japan's Kawasaki XT-4 and supersonic Mitsubishi T-2 (capable of Mach 1.6 on the power of two Rolls-Royce Turboméca Adour Mk 801A turbofan engines), Poland's recently out of production PZL Mielec TS-11 Iskra, Romanian IAR-99 Soim, Spanish CASA C-101 Aviojet, the AIDC XAT-3 from Taiwan, British BAe Hawk, and Yugoslav SOKO G2-A Galeb and new Super Galeb. Production of many of these will be limited and others may even

fail to attract major orders, leaving only a proportion to enjoy wide international success.

Many of the trainers listed are of basically similar configuration and performance, accommodating a pupil in the front cockpit and the instructor to the rear in an elevated position. Because of this similarity, just three types have been chosen here for further detailing.

The first of these is the Dassault-Breguet/Dornier-built Alpha Jet, which has enjoyed considerable success with the air forces of France and West Germany and those of several other nations including Belgium, Egypt and Morocco. First flown as a prototype in October 1973, it is powered by two SNECMA/Turboméca Larzac 04-C5 turbofan engines that are installed in the fuselage sides under the swept shoulder-mounted wings. These engines provide the aircraft with a maximum speed of 1000km/h (621mph) at sea level and allow the carriage of 2500kg (5510lb) of weapons. The basic trainer version can

use this weapon-carrying capability for training purposes or for actual light attack missions. Federal German Air Force Alpha Jets differ from those used by France and other nations by having been assigned close support and reconnaissance roles from delivery as Fiat G91R-3 replacements. The French and Federal German air forces each received 175 Alpha Jets. A new and improved close support version has also been developed recently as the Alpha Jet NGEA, which is better equipped and features a laser range-finder in a modified nose. The first two customers for the Alpha Jet NGEA were Egypt and Cameroun, the former assembling both this version and the earlier trainer at a factory at Helwan as MS2s and MS1s respectively.

The Italian Rolls-Royce Viper-engined Aermacchi MB 339A, first flown in 1976, also has a specialized attack variant, known as the MB 339K Veltro 2. However, unlike the attack versions of the Alpha Jet, this has been modified to become a single seater with a pay-

Air-to-air missile capability is also a feature of some RAF British Aerospace Hawk T.Mk 1 trainers, so equipped to perform an air defense role in time of crisis. This capability, not originally intended for the Hawk, also encouraged trials with a Sea Eagle anti-shipping missile carried under the fuselage. The Hawk, first flown in August 1974, is often acknowledged to be the world's finest trainer of its type. Powered by a single Rolls-Royce Turboméca Adour Mk 151 turbofan engine, which bestows a maximum speed of 1038km/h (645mph), it has low-mounted slightly sweptback

load capability of 1937kg (4270lb). Fixed armament comprises a 30mm DEFA cannon.

East European air forces have been served since the mid-1970s by the Czech Aero L-39 Albatros, developed as a modern replacement for the earlier L-29 Delphin. The four versions so far introduced include an attack and reconnaissance model designated L-39 ZA and the target towing L-390. Main users of the Albatros are the air forces of the Soviet Union, Czechoslovakia and East Germany, while others have been exported, making this the most produced modern jet trainer type in the world. More than 1500 have already been delivered. The straight-winged Albatros is powered by a single Ivchenko AI-25 turbofan engine, which allows a maximum speed of 755km/h (469mph). The specialized L-39 ZA has a 23mm twin-barrel cannon under the fuselage but this model, and the training versions, can also carry 1100kg (2425lb) of weapons or other underwing stores (including air-to-air missiles).

Above: The French Air Force received twenty Dassault-Breguet Mirage III-RD reconnaissance aircraft, each with OMERA cameras carried in a modified nose.

Right: Lebanese Air Force Dassault-Breguet Mirage III-EL, a version of the Mirage III-E.

wings and can carry more than 2567kg (5660lb) of weapons and other stores in a secondary attack role.

From 1976 the RAF received 175 production Hawks and others have been exported. It also forms the basis of the McDonnell Douglas/BAe Hawk VTXTS, which is to be the US Navy's new trainer under T-45 designations.

Leaving trainers aside, Europe has many varied programs underway. Some cover the continued production of aircraft that have been around for many years, while others the development of types for future military or commercial use.

Probably the best known of all French-built military aircraft is the Dassault-Breguet Mirage III, first flown in 1956 as an all-weather interceptor and day attack fighter with Mach 2 performance. Over a period of more than two decades it has been a most successful aircraft for French and foreign use, its distinctive delta wings and vertical tail configuration (and name) being adopted by Dassault-Breguet for several later designs.

Although in 1983 the production rate of the Mirage III was only some two aircraft a month, it is testament to the excellence of the design that its production period has equalled such famous aircraft as the Soviet MiG-21. Of all the many versions produced over the years for interceptor, fighter-bomber, intruder, reconnaissance and tandem two-seat training roles, the most important has been the Mirage III-E, delivered since 1964. This is a long-range fighter-bomber and intruder aircraft, powered by a single SNECMA Atar 9C turbojet. As a fighter for an

air-to-air role, armament can comprise one Matra R.530 and two Matra R.550 Magic missiles plus guns. For attack a warload of 4000kg (8818lb) is possible, which, for a small number of French Air Force aircraft of the 4e Escadre, can include tactical nuclear weapons. Armed for attack, the radius of operation is 1200km (745 miles).

As production of the Mirage III reaches its twilight period, so Dassault-Breguet has rejuvenated the aircraft in the form of the Mirage III NG (Nouvelle Génération). This retains much of the highly successful Mirage III airframe but has root extensions to the leading-edges of the wings and swept-back foreplanes aft of the cockpit. Power is provided by the greater-thrusting SNECMA Atar 9K-50 turbojet engine which, while not taking the aircraft beyond the normal Mach 2.2 maximum speed, prevents the Mirage III NG from losing performance as a consequence of a heavier weapon load and resulting higher gross weight. Another innovation is the use of a fly-by-wire control system similar to that developed for the Mirage 2000. The prototype Mirage III NG first flew towards the end of 1982 and was seen at the 1983 Paris Air Show.

More than 30 percent of the 1400-plus Mirage III/5/50 series aircraft ordered by early 1983 were Mirage 5s, a specialized ground attack derivative of the Mirage III-E featuring an increased fuel capacity for longer range, a reduced standard of avionics as appropriate to

its role, and an increase in weapon capability. As a secondary duty, the Mirage 5 can also perform as an interceptor. A faster climbing, more maneuverable and more-powerful derivative of the earlier Mirages is the Mirage 50, which appeared in 1979. Capable of all the combat roles detailed for the Mirage III series but with greater range or weapon-carrying capability, it is a true multi-mission aircraft. However, in terms of orders, so far it has not come anywhere close to the successes of earlier Mirages. The Chilean Air Force has received

examples. Lack of orders must relate to the number of newer aircraft on the international market that fulfil a similar role.

Currently the French Air Force's most important fighter is the Mirage F1, first flown in prototype form in December 1966 as a Mirage III replacement. This aircraft reiterated the company's faith in the small single-seat fighter; the official French Mirage III replacement had been requested as a larger two-seat aircraft designated F2.

Unlike all other aircraft in the Mirage series, the F1 has sweptback

Right: These Dassault-Breguet Mirage 5s were purchased by Saudi Arabia but transferred to Egypt (seen here in Saudi markings). In 1983 Egypt received 16 further aircraft as Mirage 5-E2s.

Below: SIAI-Marchetti S.211 prototypes, the nearest aircraft having been the first to fly, in April 1981.

105

wings and a tail unit incorporating an all-moving tailplane. Otherwise the F1 is generally similar to the Mirage III. It was also the first single-seat Mirage to adopt the more powerful SNECMA Atar 9K-50 turbojet, first used in the twin-engined two-seat Mirage IVA Mach 2 strategic bomber of delta configuration, which had appeared in 1959 (34 remain in operational squadron use today as low-level tactical strike aircraft).

Of nearly 700 Mirage F1s ordered by the spring of 1983, the French Air Force has been allocated 252. These comprise the F1-C interceptor, F1-B two-seat training version and the F1-R reconnaissance model. Of the F1-Cs, 25 have been modified to F1-C-200 type by the addition of removable flight refueling probes to increase their range. To date only France operates the reconnaissance variant, but a number of export F1-E multi-role aircraft have been delivered to other air forces. At high altitude the F1-C has a maximum speed of Mach 2.2. Armament for an air-to-air mission comprises two 30mm cannon plus two Matra Super 530 and two Matra 550 Magic or Sidewinder missiles. Attack weapons, up to a maximum weight of 6300kg (13,889lb), can include AS.30 Laser or AM39 Exocet missiles.

To the surprise of many onlookers, the latest Mirage for French Air Force service has reverted to the familiar delta wing and vertical tail only configuration. This is the single-seat Mirage 2000. However, the adoption of this configuration followed only after careful study of its advantages in relation to weight, simplicity of structure and performance characteristics. These, combined with the use of the latest weight-saving materials for parts of the airframe, the adoption of a fly-by-wire control system which provides artificial stability for aircraft designed for best performance rather than for pleasant handling qualities, and the selection of the SNECMA M53 turbofan (which is of higher thrust than the turbojets in earlier Mirages), have ensured that the Mirage 2000 is far superior to the aircraft it will supersede.

The first Mirage 2000 prototype made its maiden flight on 10 March 1978 and production Mirage 2000C1 interceptors began entering French Air Force in 1983. It is expected that 200 will eventually be acquired by this force for interceptor duties, each capable of a maximum speed and range with auxiliary fuel of Mach 2.3+ and 1850km (1149 miles) respectively. In addition to the standard two 30mm cannon, two Matra Super 530 and two Magic or a total of four Magic air-to-air missiles can be carried.

Above: The Mirage 50 is a multimission fighter.

Above: Three prototype Dassault-Breguet Mirage 2000s are made to look small alongside the larger Super Mirage 4000 prototype.

Below: One of the 34 Dassault-Breguet Mirage IVA two-seat tactical strike aircraft that remain in operational squadron use with the French Air Force.

Above: Two of the 25 Dassault-Breguet Mirage F1-C-200s operated by the 5e Escadre at Orange, armed with Matra 550 Magic (wingtips) and Matra R.530 air-to-air missiles.

Already Egypt, Abu Dhabi, Peru and India have selected the Mirage 2000 for service, all of which except India have been operators of the Mirage III and/or Mirage 5. In addition, Dassault-Breguet has developed the Mirage 2000B two-seat trainer and the two-seat Mirage 2000N low-altitude penetration/strike variant. The first French order for the 'N' was placed in 1983. The total stores load that can be carried externally by the 'N' is 6000kg (13,228lb). The French aircraft will include provision for the ASMP tactical nuclear missile. The first production deliveries will begin in 1986. A future Mirage 2000 variant must take in the role of reconnaissance.

Having been successful in the past in developing private venture combat aircraft that attracted French and foreign orders, Dassault-Breguet has gone ahead with the construction of a more ambitious multi-role combat delta prototype which is known as the Mirage 4000. Considerably larger than the Mirage 2000 and yet still a single seater, it features two M53 engines, a fly-by-wire control system, swept foreplanes to the rear of the new-style canopy, and has a radar offering far greater search

range. It has a maximum speed of Mach 2.3+ and a combat radius while carrying auxiliary fuel and an external store of about 1850km (1149 miles). To date no orders are known to have been placed.

The French Navy still operates both the Dassault-Breguet Etendard IV-M strike fighter and the IV-P reconnaissance variant, but their importance has been downgraded since it took delivery of 71 improved Super Etendards from 1978. The Super Etendard transonic strike fighter made world press in 1982 when eight of the fourteen ordered for export to Argentina were used in action against British Task Force ships during the Falkland Islands conflict, each aircraft being capable of launching the deadly Exocet anti-shipping missile. One of these aircraft/missile combinations brought about the destruction of HMS *Sheffield*, a Type 42 destroyer, on 4 May that year. Since that time Iraq has also received Super Etendard/Exocets, delivered in the latter part of 1983.

The Super Etendard was designed to supersede the Etendard as a carrier-based aircraft with a maximum speed for low altitude missions of 1180km/h (733mph). It is conventional in configuration, with swept wings and tail surfaces and is powered by a single SNECMA Atar 8K-50 turbojet. Apart

from two 30mm cannon, its weapon load is fairly light at 2100kg (4630lb), indicating the importance of its ability to carry Exocet or tactical nuclear weapons. It can also undertake fighter missions carrying Magic missiles. French Navy aircraft are at sea only on the carrier *Clemenceau*, although *Foch* too can be so equipped.

Dassault-Breguet is also very well known for its range of twin-turbofan executive jets, which can be delivered alternatively with interior changes to permit a range of other civil and military duties. The former Mystère-Falcon 10 and 20 have been superseded by the four- to seven-passenger Mystère-Falcon 100 and nine- to twelve-passenger Mystère-Falcon 200, both with Garrett turbofan engines mounted on the rear fuselage. Maritime surveillance derivatives are the Mystère-Falcon 20G, operated by the US Coast Guard as the HU-25A Guardian, and the Gardian for the French Navy. A longer range executive jet with accommodation for eight to twelve passengers (or freight, as for the other transports in the range) is the Mystère-Falcon 50. Powered by three Garrett TFE731-3 turbofan engines, this has a maximum speed of 648km/h (402mph) and a range with eight passengers of 6480km (4025 miles). A new Dassault-Breguet trijet executive aircraft with intercontinental

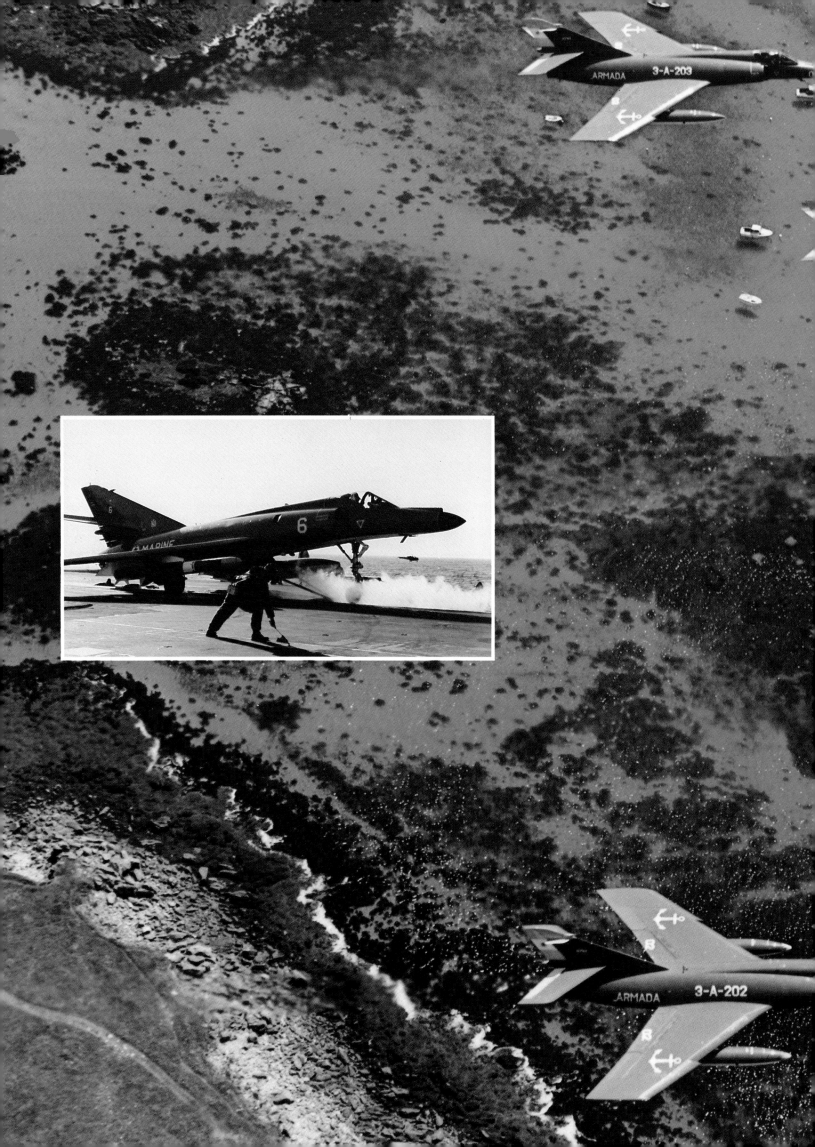

range is expected to become available in 1986 as the Mystère-Falcon 900.

Britain's representative in the field of business jets has been for many years the British Aerospace (formerly Hawker Siddeley) HS 125. The latest version is the Series 800, which differs from previous models by having a redesigned interior and a new flight deck incorporating an electronic flight instrument system. Power is provided by two Garrett TFE731-5R-1H engines, mounted on the rear of the fuselage. However, to date the best selling version has been the Series 700, first flown in

1976. This version, with accommodation for eight to fourteen passengers and powered by TFE731-3-1RH turbofans, has a maximum cruising speed of 808km/h (502mph) and a range with full load of 4482km (2785 miles).

Since the end of BAe One-Eleven production in Britain – although this airliner is currently being manufactured under license in Romania as the IAv Bucuresti Rombac 1-11 in Series 495 (up to 89 passengers) and Series 560 (lengthened for up to 109 passengers) versions – the future of Britain's indigenous manufacture of airliners has

rested on the BAe 146. This uniquely configured short-range airliner has already entered scheduled services, inaugurated on 27 May 1983 by Dan-Air using the 71- to 93-seat Series 100 and on 27 June 1983 by Air Wisconsin with the lengthened and longer-range 82-109 passenger Series 200. Both versions are powered by four Avco Lycoming ALF 502R-3 turbofan engines, carried in pods under the high-lift aerofoil section wings. Other differences between the versions include the ability of the Series 100 to operate from semi-prepared airstrips of short length. Maximum cruising speed for both versions is 778km/h (483mph), while the Series 200 has a range of 1853km (1150 miles) with the maximum payload.

Inset, previous page: A French Navy Dassault-Breguet Super Etendard.

Previous page: An Argentine Navy Super Etendard sank HMS *Sheffield* during the Falklands conflict.

Left: Three executive jets of the Mystère-Falcon range have been the triple-engined 50 (right) and the twin-turbofan 20 and 10.

Right: The latest version of the highly successful BAe HS 125, the Series 800.

Below: The BAe One-Eleven is currently only produced in Romania, as the Rombac 1-11.

Inset right: The first BAe 146 Series 200 was put into service by Air Wisconsin in mid-1983.

Above: The world's only supersonic airliner currently in regular service is the Anglo-French Concorde, seen here in the livery of British Airways.

Inset: A major operator of the European Airbus A300 is Thai International.

Left: The prototype Airbus A310 took to the air for the first time in April 1982. Production A310s have since gone to Swissair and Lufthansa.

Britain, of course, has been a partner with France in the Concorde program, which once promised to revolutionize air transport (with, at one time, a large number of purchasing options held by airlines from around the world). In the event only 16 production Concordes were built, all making their first flights between December 1973 and April 1979 and seven going into service with Air France and seven with British Airways. Currently, and probably for a long period to come, Concorde is the world's only supersonic airliner in regular commercial use. Despite the small number in service, it is the most advanced airliner in the world, its Mach 2.04 maximum cruising speed making it as fast as many fighters. Accommodation is provided for 100 passengers, and with maximum payload it has a range of up to 6230km (3870 miles). The air-

liner's most important routes have always been those to America: New York services were inaugurated from Paris by Air France and London by British Airways on 22 November 1977.

Britain is currently working with the other nations mentioned at the beginning of this chapter on the production and development of the Airbus A300 and A310 European wide-bodied airliners. Despite fairly slow sales initially, both models are now very well established in airline service and production continues to meet orders that had totaled 248 A300s and 108 A310s by August 1983.

The A300 is a short- to medium-range airliner that was unique, until the introduction of Boeing's Model 767, by being a wide-bodied transport with only two large turbofan engines (General Electric CF6-50 series or Pratt & Whitney JT9D-59 series initially). The first production version was the A300B2 (now A300B2-100), delivered for commercial use from 1974. The B2, currently available in several models including the more advanced A300B2-600 version with increased payload and engine options including the Rolls-Royce RB.211-524D4 and Pratt & Whitney PW4058, was followed by the longer-range B-4 and variants. These

now include the more advanced A300B4-600. The Airbus A300C4 is a convertible freighter variant of the B4, suitable for up to 315 passengers, a mixed passenger/cargo load or all cargo. A freighter only is the A300F4. Accommodation in the A300B2 and B4 is provided for up to 336 passengers, while the maximum cruising speed is 911km/h (567mph). Range of the A300B4-100 with 269 passengers on board is 4910km (3050 miles).

The Airbus A310 was evolved from the A300 and differs mainly in two respects. Firstly it has new advanced technology wings of smaller span and reduced area, again the work of British Aerospace, while the fuselage has been shortened to a length of 46.66m (153ft 1in), compared to the A300's 53.62m (175ft 11in). This provides accommodation for a maximum of only 280 passengers or a smaller amount of freight. Other changes include a new tailplane. Four versions of the A310 are currently on offer, comprising the A310-200 passenger version and the longer-range A310-300 for use from 1986, the A310C-200 convertible and A310F-200 freighter. The third of Airbus Industrie's current programs covers the much smaller 147- to 179-passenger A320, due for service from 1988.

Apart from the Hawk trainer, mentioned earlier, British Aerospace has several types of military jet in production for the home services and for export. From the Nimrod, a maritime anti-submarine patrol aircraft based upon the Comet 4C airframe and delivered to the RAF in MR.Mk 1 (43 aircraft, all but 11 assigned for conversion to more advanced MR.Mk 2 form) and R.Mk 1 electronic intelligence (three aircraft) forms, British Aerospace has developed an early warning variant known as the Nimrod AEW.Mk 3. Fourteen AEW.Mk 3s,

converted from Nimrod MR.Mk 1s plus the three development aircraft, are to join the RAF, the first of which entered service in 1983. Each of these aircraft is distinctively configured by having scanners housed in huge bulges to the nose and tail of the fuselage, the nose position being merged into the maritime Nimrod's underfuselage pannier which would otherwise house the bomb bay, radome and other equipment. The mission for the Nimrod AEW.Mk 3 is much the same as those for the AWACS aircraft operated by NATO, the USA, the USSR and other nations.

The Falklands conflict of 1982 brought to world attention a number of aircraft both old and new, but none more so than the Royal Navy's British Aerospace Sea Harrier FRS.Mk 1 and the RAF's Harrier GR.Mk 3. Developed from a series of prototype and development V/STOL aircraft known as P.1127s and Kestrels, the first of which made its maiden flight in 1966, the Harrier became the first operational fixed-wing V/STOL aircraft in the world when it entered RAF service in its original GR.Mk 1 form in 1969.

The secret of the Harrier's success lies in its Rolls-Royce Pegasus vectored-thrust turbofan engine, which in the RAF's current Harrier GR.Mk 3 version is a Mk 103. The exhaust from this engine is directed to the rear for horizontal flight, or through varying angles up to 98° from the fully-aft position, by four rotatable nozzles. Vertical take-off is, therefore, achieved with these nozzles in downward facing position, while STOL (short take off and landing) is also easily within the capability of

Left: Nimrod MR.Mk 2s at BAe Manchester before redelivery into RAF service, each sporting a refueling probe above the cockpit.

Below: The unmistakable Nimrod AEW.Mk 3, carrying scanners in two huge bulges at the nose and tail of the fuselage.

Above: A Royal Navy Sea Harrier FRS.Mk 1, photographed before the Falklands conflict, in VTOL flight over a carrier deck.

Left: Four of the RAF's British Aerospace Harrier GR.Mk 3s operated during the Falklands conflict flew directly from the UK to Ascension Island using inflight refueling and then, after a brief stopover, flew on eventually to land on the deck of the Royal Navy carrier HMS *Hermes*.

the Harrier. STOL performance is particularly useful when the situation allows, as a heavier weapon load can be carried. With the Pegasus vectored thrust turbofan, no other lift-jets are required.

The Harrier can carry a normal maximum external load of 2270kg (5000lb). The two-seat training variants in service with all Harrier/Sea Harrier operating nations are also capable of carrying the full load. Other users of the Harrier are the US Marine Corps – which operates single-seat AV-8As, upgraded AV-8Cs and TAV-8A two-seaters – and the Spanish Navy which has a small number of single-seat AV-8S Matadors and TAV-8S two-seaters for operation from the aircraft carrier *Dedalo*. US and Spanish Harriers were delivered with the ability to carry Sidewinder air-to-air missiles, and RAF Harriers used in the Falklands conflict were retrospectively given this capability.

In 1975 the British government finalized its plans to proceed with full development of a carrier-borne fighter/reconnaissance/strike variant of the Harrier for the Royal Navy, known as the Sea Harrier. The intention was that five Sea Harriers would be operated from each light aircraft carrier of the new *Invincible* class, together with nine Westland Sea King anti-submarine helicopters. These carriers were to replace the last of the Royal Navy's large aircraft carriers deploying fixed-wing aircraft (Phantom II fighters and Bucanneer two-seat low-level strike

115

Inset left: A Sidewinder-carrying Sea Harrier FRS.Mk 1 in combat colors.

Inset right: The first Sea Harrier FRS.Mk 51 for the Indian Navy is rolled out during a ceremony.

Main picture: RAF Harriers in special camouflage for exercises in snow conditions in Europe.

aircraft). This decision was not welcomed in all circles, many people expressing doubts as to the Sea Harrier's suitability as a fighter to supersede the much faster and longer-range Phantom II.

The first Sea Harrier, designated FRS.Mk 1 for the Royal Navy, flew initially on 20 August 1978 and sea trials were carried out on the converted old style anti-submarine carrier HMS *Hermes*. This vessel was given a 'ski jump' at the end of its flight deck, an idea conceived to assist STOL take-off with the Sea Harrier at higher gross weight. On 11 June 1980 the first of the Royal Navy's new carriers, HMS *Invincible*, was commissioned, this too having a ski jump. With other vessels of the class under construction and the government wanting to cut defense expenditure, HMS *Invincible* was offered for sale to Australia at a knockdown rate, a sale confirmed on 24 February 1982. Then, on 2 April that year, Argentine forces invaded the Falkland Islands. With no progress being achieved through the United Nations to settle the dispute, the main elements of a British Task Force set sail for the South Atlantic, its vessels including HMS *Hermes* and *Invincible*, each carrying more Sea Harriers than originally intended.

On 1 May the Sea Harrier proved itself as a combat plane, when nine attacked the airfield at Port Stanley and three the airstrip at Goose Green, while in air-to-air combat the first of the Sea Harriers' many victories was gained over an Argentine Mirage IIIEA fighter-bomber. During the conflict, which ended on 14 June, the 28 Sea Harriers operated performed 2380 missions. None was destroyed in air-to-air combat, although five were lost to accidents and ground fire. The only British prisoner of war was a 'downed' Sea Harrier pilot. Much of the Sea Harrier's impressive air-to-air combat record was due to the aircraft's ability to use its vectored-thrust engine to perform outstanding maneuvers. Today HMS *Invincible* has been joined by *Illustrious* and the new *Ark Royal*.

The Sea Harrier differs from the Harrier in several ways. Firstly the Sea Harrier carries a nose-mounted Ferranti multi-mode radar in a pointed nosecone to suit its air-to-air role, while the RAF's Harrier has a 'thimble' nose housing a laser ranger and marked target seeker for precision attacks on ground targets. Other differences include a Mk 104 turbofan engine, the pilot seated in a raised position under a blister-type cockpit canopy, and weapon options including as standard two Sidewinder missiles. Maximum speed and radius of action for a high-altitude interception mission are 1185km/h (736mph) and 750km (460 miles) respectively. The second Sea Harrier-operating nation is India, whose Navy has received a small number of FRS.Mk 51s.

A very important tactical support aircraft with the RAF is the Jaguar. Although not possessing the Harrier's ability to move up with ground forces and hide in natural cover due to its VTOL capability, the Jaguar can fly supersonically at sea level or at Mach 1.6 at high altitude and deliver a heavy attack at a radius of 537-917km (334-570 miles). The RAF received 165 Jaguar GR.Mk 1 single seaters (Jaguar S version) and 38 two-seat training Jaguar T.Mk 2s (Jaguar B version). The French Air Force, whose aircraft can carry tactical nuclear weapons as an alternative to the normal bombs, rockets, missiles and other stores up to a weight of 4535kg (10,000lb), received 160 single-seat Jaguar As and 40 two-seat Jaguar E trainers.

The Jaguar was developed and is built by an international company known as SEPECAT, which is run by British Aerospace and Dassault/Breguet. Currently the only version in production in Europe is the Jaguar International, the export version. Powered by either two Rolls-Royce Turboméca Adour Mk 804 turbofans (equivalent in power to the RAF's Adour Mk 104 engine) or more powerful Adour Mk 811s, the International has the best performance and maneuverability of all Jaguar variants. According to the requirements of the customer, armament can include overwing pylons for air-to-air missiles or anti-shipping missiles carried under the wings and fuselage (including Exocet and Harpoon). Countries operating Jaguar Internationals include India (now built under license at Bangalore), Ecuador and Oman.

A similar aircraft to the Jaguar has been developed by SOKO of Yugoslavia and CNIAR of Romania for their home air forces. Known as the Orao in Yugoslavia and IAR-93 in Romania, it is a single-seat close support and attack aircraft with interceptor capability but is also being produced in two-seat training form. The first production examples flew in 1981. The Romanian Air Force is to receive 165 IAR-93Bs and twenty less powerful IAR-93As, each using two license-built examples of the Rolls-Royce Viper turbojet engine (non afterburning for the IAR-93As). Each version covers both single- and two-seat models. Production quantities for the Yugoslav Air Force are probably to be similar. Like the Jaguar, the Orao/IAR-93 has two cannon as fixed armament, but its maximum weapon and stores load is only 1500kg (3307lb). Maximum speed of the IAR-93B is about 1160km/h (721mph) and its radius of action with a 1000kg (2205lb) bombload and an auxiliary fuel tank is about 530km (329 miles).

Yet another European program has produced the Panavia Tornado, which is the first variable-geometry combat aircraft to join the RAF, the West

German Luftwaffe and Marineflieger, and the Italian Air Force. The IDS (interdictor strike) is the main version of the Tornado, intended to equip all the services mentioned earlier. The RAF has so far acquired more than 100 of the 220 IDS Tornados it is eventually to receive, these having taken over from the Vulcan as strike aircraft. Other roles will include reconnaissance. As the Tornado GR.Mk 1, to give it its RAF designation, becomes more established, the Buccaneer's land and maritime strike roles will be taken over also. In addition, the RAF is to receive the only air-defense variants of the Tornado built, 165 of which will eventually replace Lightnings and Phantom IIs. This version, RAF designated Tornado F.Mk 2, will also be a two seater.

The Luftwaffe is in the process of receiving 212 IDS Tornados for battlefield interdiction, close support and offensive/defensive use against potential enemy aircraft in a role known as counter air. West German Navy (Marineflieger) units are also receiving the IDS version, its 112 aircraft being assigned naval strike and reconnaissance duties. Just over half the 100 IDS Tornados assigned for the Italian Air Force will be operational as ground attack, reconnaissance and air superiority aircraft, the rest either performing a training role or are designated reserve aircraft.

First flown as a prototype on 14 August 1974, the Tornado is a Mach 2.2 combat plane, powered by two Turbo-Union RB.199-34R Mk 101 turbofan engines. It has fixed armament of two 27mm cannon and can carry up to about 8165kg (18,000lb) of non-nuclear weapons in IDS form. With a heavy weapon load this version has a combat radius of about 1390km (863 miles),

making it a very able warplane. However, it is a far lighter aircraft than the USAF's F-111 or the Soviet Su-24 swing-wing attack aircraft, which have longer ranges and nuclear capability. Armament for the RAF's Tornado F.Mk 2 is one cannon plus four Sky Flash and two Sidewinder air-to-air missiles.

The British developed Sky Flash, a Mach 4 missile with a range of 50km (31 miles) based upon the American Sparrow, is also a main weapon (with the Sidewinder) of the JA 37 single-seat interceptor version of the Swedish Saab Viggen, the only variant still in production. The Viggen, first flown as a prototype in early 1967, is a multi-mission aircraft of very distinctive

Top: An IDS Tornado in German Luftwaffe service, used by a weapon conversion unit.

Above: Saab JA 37 interceptor of the F13 Wing at Norrköping in the new camouflage colors.

Left: Preproduction CNIAR IAR-93 close support aircraft, built in Romania.

Right: The RAF is the only service to receive the air defense variant (ADV) of the Tornado. A prototype F.Mk 2 is seen here demonstrating its maneuverability to the camera.

Inset: An early Panavia Tornado refuels an RAF Tornado GR.Mk 1 using a buddy-buddy refueling pack.

configuration. It has delta-type rear-mounted wings with compound leading-edge sweep and forward fuselage foreplanes. This configuration, once unique to the Viggen, is fast becoming the adopted style the world over for light

combat aircraft for the 1990s. Power is provided by a single Volvo Flygmotor RM8 series turbofan, which is a supersonic military development of the civil Pratt & Whitney JT8D engine.

Earlier production versions of the Viggen, of which the Swedish Air Force received 180 examples, were the AJ 37 all-weather attack aircraft with interceptor capability, the SF 37 photographic reconnaissance model, the SH 37 maritime reconnaissance version and the SK 37 tandem two-seat trainer with attack capability. Both reconnaissance models can be armed with air-to-air missiles if required for defense. Like these versions, the JA 37 interceptor can also perform a secondary role, for a ground attack mission

carrying perhaps six 135mm rockets in each of four pods. However, primary armament for this Mach 2+ aircraft is one 30mm long-range cannon plus four Sidewinder and two Sky Flash missiles. The combat radius of the JA 37 can be 1000km (620 miles).

Another aircraft that made its maiden flight in 1967 is the Fokker F28 Fellowship short- to medium-range airliner. More than 200 had been ordered for commercial and military use by the summer of 1983, the two current versions available being the 65-passenger or VIP F28 Mk 3000 and the longer 85-passenger Mk 4000. Both, as for previous versions, use major assemblies produced by Fokker itself, MBB in Germany and Shorts in the UK and are

powered by two rear-mounted Rolls-Royce RB.183-2 Mk 555-15P turbofan engines. Maximum cruising speed is 843km/h (523mph) at a gross weight of 29,000kg (63,935lb) and range of the Mk 4000 with a full passenger load is 2085km (1295 miles).

Below: The Fokker F28 Fellowship is to be found in commercial and military service, this Mk 3000 serving as a VIP transport with the Ghana Air Force.

Right: The original version of the IAI Kfir multi-mission fighter was followed by the Kfir-C2, changes made to improve performance and low-speed maneuverability including the adoption of foreplanes.

Below right: The IAI Westwind 2 was developed to offer better range and operating costs than the Westwind 1.

Outside of Europe, the USA, USSR and China, few nations produce or have recently built what can really be termed modern jet aircraft. Certainly countries like India have an impressive record of constructing aircraft under license that originated abroad but these do not count. Nor can India's HAL Ajeet single-seat lightweight interceptor and attack aircraft be included, as it was based on the Gnat fighter developed in the 1950s by Folland Aircraft of the UK.

Israel's first attempt at producing its own fighter resulted in the IAI Nesher, which was based on the Israeli-operated Mirage III and first flew in prototype form in 1969. The Nesher became operational from 1972 and about 40 were available for use during the Yom Kippur War of 1973. Israel had also developed by then its own dogfight missile as the Rafael Shafrir. Twenty-six exported Neshers were in service with Argentina during the conflict over the Falkland Islands in 1982.

By 1973, however, Israel had gone one step further in making itself less dependent on French combat planes

and spares, by producing the prototype of a more advanced interceptor-fighter and ground attack aircraft known as the IAI Kfir. Unlike the Nesher, which used the French SNECMA Atar 9C turbojet engine, the Kfir was designed to use a General Electric J79 turbojet, but retained the delta wings and vertical tail only configuration of the Mirage III/5/Nesher.

The original production version of the Kfir was superseded by the Kfir-C2. The most obvious of several changes made to improve the aircraft's performance at take off and lower-speed maneuverability was the adoption of foreplanes, which can be removed when these performance characteristics are not of paramount importance to the mission. Maximum speed and radius of action for the Kfir-C2 are Mach 2.3+ and up to 776km (482 miles) with auxiliary fuel and two air-to-air missiles respectively. Armament choices for ground attack, in addition to the aircraft's fixed 30mm cannon, can include the Israeli-built Luz-1 missile (intended primarily to destroy antiaircraft weapon systems) or other air-to-surface

missiles, bombs and so on. A two-seat training variant of the Kfir-C2 is the Kfir-TC2. Kfir-C2s have also been supplied to Colombia. Even more advanced versions of the Kfir, first mentioned in 1983, are the single-seat Kfir-C7 and TC7 two seater, said to have improvements in weapon capability/range and incorporating new avionics. Total Kfir series production for home use and export must be well over 200 aircraft.

Other products of IAI (Israel Aircraft Industries) are the 1124 Westwind I, a twin Garrett turbofan-powered business jet with accommodation for ten passengers, the Sea Scan armed maritime derivative suited to a number of roles, the improved and longer range Westwind 2 business jet with new wings incorporating winglets, and the 1125 Astra. The Astra is the latest of IAI's business jets and first flew as a prototype in 1984. Powered by two Garrett TFE731-3B-100G turbofan engines, it differs from the Westwinds mainly by having newly designed and low-mounted sweptback wings and a higher standard of comfort for the six to nine passengers. Maximum cruising speed is about 876km/h (545mph) and its range with five passengers could be 6180km (3840 miles).

Japan is another country that, like India and others, has benefited from the licensed production of foreign aircraft. However, it has also produced several aircraft of its own, including the Mitsubishi T-2 tandem two-seat supersonic trainer, previously mentioned. From the T-2, which was Japan's first indigenous supersonic aircraft, Mitsubishi developed the F-1 single-seat close support fighter for the JASDF. By the spring of 1983 that force had received 66 F-1s of 71 ordered to date. Each F-1 is powered by two Rolls-Royce Turboméca Adour Mk 801A turbofan engines and differs mainly from the T-2 in having a fairing over the rear cockpit area, various changes to the avionics and equipment, and armament comprising the standard 20mm cannon plus four Sidewinder air-to-air missiles or up to 2721kg (6000lb) of ground attack weapons. An important F-1 weapon is the Mitsubishi ASM-1, used by the JASDF as the Type 80 anti-shipping missile. The F-1 can carry two Type 80s and to date is the only aircraft to be so equipped.

Another Japanese aircraft manufacturer satisfied the JASDF requirement for a Curtiss C-46 commando transport replacement, when between 1974 and 1981 Kawasaki delivered 29 C-1 medium-range transports. Each is powered by two Mitsubishi-built Pratt & Whitney JT8D-M-9 turbofan engines. Accommodation is provided for 60 troops or fewer paratroops/stretchers, or up to 11,900kg (26,235lb) of freight, vehicles or a 105mm howitzer. Maximum speed of the C-1 is more than 800km/h (500mph) and range with a 7900kg (17,416lb) load is 1300km (808 miles).

Already aircraft manufacturers/bureaus around the world are working towards the new aircraft for the 1990s and the next century. The future trend for military combat aircraft is undoubtedly towards smaller and lighter multi-role types, constructed from advanced composite materials. The weapon carrying capability of such aircraft will be so good that larger fighter-bombers or heavy bombers will only be required when long-range is an operational necessity. Future aircraft may well use more aspects of low observable technology, resulting in very different airframes with most angles smoothed out, engines and intakes in new positions, and new materials used and special paint applied to reduce specular reflection or, more simply, the radar echo signature given off by an aircraft. Changes to the general configuration of transport aircraft are likely to be less obvious, although the future main power plant could be the propfan, basically a turboprop driving a very advanced multi-blade propeller.

Inset: From its T-2 supersonic trainer, Mitsubishi developed the F-1 single-seat close support fighter for use by the JASDF.

Below: As a replacement for the JASDF's old Curtiss Commando transports, Kawasaki developed the thoroughly modern C-1.

Following page: A Boeing 747.

INDEX

Page numbers in italics refer to illustrations

Acknowledgments
The photographs in this book
are from the author's collection
with the exception of the
following:
Dennis Hughes 24/5, 89 (below),
90 (below)
Imperial War Museum 18/19
Bob Snyder 14/15
USAF 12/13, 23